M000197065

THE
THRIVER'S
TOOLBOX

THE
THRIVER'S
TOOLB⚙X

From the Teachings of
Ralph Sarway

Written by
Isaac J. Kassin

PART I

THE THRIVER'S TOOLBOX

All rights are reserved. No part of this book may be used or reproduced in any manner whatsoever without the written permission of the copyright owner except for the use of quotations in book reviews.

Copyright © 2020 Isaac J. Kassin

First edition May 2020

(Paperback) ISBN: 978-1-946274-50-2
(e-book) ISBN: 978-1-946274-51-9

Library of Congress Control Number: 2020939007

[2 3 4 5 6 7 8 9 10]

Jacket design by Okomota
Interior Design: Amit Dey
Published by Wordeee in the United States, Beacon, New York 2020

Website: www.wordeee.com
Twitter: wordeeeupdates
Facebook: facebook.com/wordeee/
e-Mail: contact@wordeee.com

"The journey of a thousand miles starts with a single step."

— **Lao Tzu**

TABLE OF CONTENTS

PREFACE

I WALK INTO a dimly lit bar and look for the last booth by the window. I find it. He's sitting there, smiling unassumingly, and waves me over. A very close friend of mine told me I must meet him. Supposedly he's a guru, a legend of sorts, who coaches people of all types, from billionaires to children, on how to become their greatest selves. He teaches them how to "thrive." My buddy insisted I meet him, so I gave him a call and scheduled an appointment. He sent me the address of a bar I'd never heard of. I was told he meets in open, comfortable settings only, like bars, restaurants, and hotel lobbies. That sounded cool, so I let him pick the place. It was a great atmosphere.

We dove into conversation almost immediately, covering topics like business and philosophy. After discovering that I was an avid reader, he asked me what my two favorite books of all time were. I shared them with him (*Think and Grow Rich* and *The Alchemist* at the time), which also happened to be his favorite two! We hit it off.

After an hour, he began to ask personal questions. Comfortable and confident discussing most things about myself, I answered them while he listened intently. Once I finished, it was his turn to speak. And he blew my mind.

He started to spill endless wisdom that resonated with me and connected with my deeper self. It required an open mind, but I naturally entered conversations, receptive to new ideas and thoughts. I was engaged.

Quickly, I felt I needed to write down his words, so I started to scribble on a bar napkin. When I ran out of space, I grabbed another one. And another. After two hours of this dialogue, it was time to go. We shook hands, finished our drinks, and hoped to reconnect. Wow! What an experience.

That week, I couldn't stop thinking about our conversation. The truth he spoke. The perspective. So, I gave him a call. This time, I picked the place, and I came prepared. I bought a red Moleskine notebook and brought it along.

*   *   *

It's been almost three years since that day at the bar. Today, Ralph is a best friend of mine, and we have had hundreds of conversations over countless dinners, drinks, hangouts, and even a snowboarding trip. I spent the entire day before my wedding ceremony with him.

This book contains a lot of Ralph's secrets and principles that came from our many conversations over the years. This book, Part I, includes ideas from my bar napkins and the red notebook that I bought after that first meeting. This first part covers only the fundamentals. The parts to come will reveal more.

I decided to expand on Ralph's teachings and to publish this book because I believe these priceless tools, strategies, and techniques can help anyone, and everyone, thrive in their lives. His lessons are universal and help to equip a person with tools to optimize themselves. We're all human, with goals, dreams, hopes, and fears. Among these, we all want to be better and become our greatest selves. While we may know the end that we want, we don't always know what tools to use to get us there. Ralph provides these tools, and we can all use them to become who we aspire to become. It's a chance we all deserve. Here, I hope to get our readers started. I hope to give people access to the resources we should all have to understand ourselves more and how we could grow. All I ask is that you keep an open mind and an open heart. Be curious. Invite these new ideas and thoughts. As you read, apply the methods to your life. The more you practice and the more you implement, the more you will flourish. The more you act, the more you will see results.

With that, I welcome you to Part I of The Thriver's Toolbox and wish you all a wonderful journey on your path to thriving.

Isaac J. Kassin

FOREWORD

WHEN I SIT WITH a client for the first time, I always ask the same thing, "What do you want for your life?" People of all ages–parents, grandparents, children, teachers, politicians, business people, and thought-leaders–all have to answer this same question. Their responses? All different. Except for one part; they want to thrive.

I have personally coached hundreds of people since I started my career, and it's been quite a journey. From children struggling with anxiety issues to billionaires dealing with marital problems, I have pretty much dealt with it all. Clinical patients with psychological disorders like OCD and physiological illnesses, such as multiple sclerosis, have reversed their diagnoses using my tools. I am not a healer, nor a doctor, nor a psychiatrist. I am a tool. And I help people thrive.

Most people become confused and ask me if I'm a therapist. I am not! In fact, I am very different from a therapist. Let me explain. Therapists focus on a person's past while I focus on a person's future. Therapists train others to cope with struggle, whereas I teach people to prosper with struggle. While therapists concentrate on reconciling one topic, I work on optimizing all parts of a person's life. If my client's pressing challenge is health, we focus on that priority and then move onto the next. Eventually, a person graduates from their therapist. I train my clients through all of life.

I equip them with tools to better manage stress and anxiety, fitness and nutrition, religion and spirituality, negotiating and public speaking, and marriage and parenting. No matter what my clients are looking to optimize or excel at, I provide them with the means to better prepare themselves and to thrive.

This book in front of you is a toolbox. It is only Part I, but it contains many of my most excellent techniques and strategies for dealing with everyday challenges and opportunities. Its author, Isaac J. Kassin, is a very dear friend of mine and a brilliant researcher. He has fused my teachings with his thorough research, vivid storytelling, and articulate writing to bring my lessons to life.

Here is where I ask you, "What do you want for your life? Who do you want to be? What will be your story?"

Read these pages and think about all that. Because it's all within your grasp. This is your life. This is your story. It's time for you to thrive.

Ralph Sarway
Life Coach

INTRODUCTION

THIS BOOK is a place we can go to explore what it takes, what it means, and how to live as Thrivers. Together, we will become the best versions of ourselves that we can be at this very moment. We will focus on achieving our goals, living by our values and work towards building a better experience for ourselves and those around us. It is important to note that we are not only aspiring to thrive through positive aspects of life but also through the difficult times. We will thrive through our challenges together using the set of tools that we examine throughout this book, and we will grow even through pain, suffering, and tough times.

When life is going well, we will enjoy what we have and strive for more. We will acknowledge our accomplishments, but also search for more opportunities to grow. We will live by example and take risks when doing what we believe to be true. We will be engaged in our hobbies, work and spend time doing what is fulfilling for us. Although humble, we will stand proudly and share our joy and accomplishments with others. We will cultivate strong relationships and look to give back whenever we can. We will be grateful for our abilities to influence and understand that we must continue earning the privilege to do so. As Thrivers, we will take on responsibilities with confidence and search for meaning in all that we do.

When life is challenging, we ultimately have faith that we will prevail. We will understand the natural and inevitable pain that comes with living and stay determined to make it through. We realize that there are outside forces that can bring us suffering, and we will remain determined not to lose ourselves in the chaos. We will cry, we will feel fear and anxiety, but we will handle the emotions so well that we do not disrupt our missions or our abilities to think clearly. We will acknowledge the areas where we are weak and deliberately work towards improving. We recognize our flaws and faults, but will look at failures and criticism as opportunities for growth. We will not be afraid to learn, and we will remain resilient during setbacks. The struggle is necessary, and we will understand that effort is essential in mastering the craft of life.

The reality is, in everyone lies the ability to be a Thriver. We have all experienced moments of thriving. Some of us have performed for a large crowd – whether singing, dancing, or playing an instrument. Many of us have received a high score on an exam and felt proud of it. For those of us who are athletes, in certain games, we were in flow states and played exceptionally well. We have all felt these moments where we dominated, where we transcended our day-to-day limitations and felt powerful, where we entered a state of focus and forgot about time and our life problems. Those moments proved to us that we are capable, strong and that we have endless potential. These moments are moments of thriving.

The premise of our conversation today is not that we are not Thrivers. We have all thrived at points in our lives and felt empowered. We are merely "sleeping Thrivers," aiming to thrive more and stay thriving throughout our journeys of life. Our mission is to become Thrivers in all areas of our life, at all periods of life. We will aim to thrive through the dark times and the bright times, the tough times and the thrilling times. We must first recognize that we have what it takes to thrive and that we are gifted in areas of life that we have not tapped into yet. There are better, stronger, more capable versions of ourselves waiting to awaken. These versions of us are comfortable with fear and uncertainty; these versions can make hard and smart decisions confidently and can accomplish our goals and desires with courage. The best part— these versions of us already exist. We just need to take the first step towards being Thrivers.

THE FOUR PILLARS OF THRIVING

Becoming a Thriver involves mastering certain skills which we have broken down into the following Four Pillars:

Pillar I: A Strong Mind

A strong mind is the foundation on which the other three pillars lie. It is the first step in commanding our lives. We will develop the ability to deal with and adequately handle intrusive and negative thoughts, as well as any mental activity that weakens our wellbeing. We will learn to control and manage these thoughts. On the other side of the coin, we will develop a growth mindset. A growth mindset adheres to a method of positive thinking that strengthens the mind and allows it to become our ally rather than our opponent. Our mind should be our greatest ally rather than our biggest distraction. A strong mind enables us to manage through tough times, empowers us to take positive actions, and allows us to enjoy the pleasures in life.

Pillar II: Effective Execution

Once our minds are strong, our next objective is to set smart goals for ourselves and to execute on our ambitions. Here we learn how to implement healthy habits and to rid ourselves of destructive ones. Pillar II is about positioning ourselves to make the right decisions in our lives and to do what we know to be true.

Pillar III: Mastering Modalities

As we execute and achieve our ambitions, we will assume many roles and responsibilities. This will require operating in many modes at different times. Learning how to compartmentalize them is critical to thriving. Pillar III teaches us how to discipline ourselves to be present in the moment and to better focus on the immediate. When we are in work mode, we will be focused on work and will not daydream about our plans for the evening. When we are home having dinner with our families, we will not feel distracted and sit obsessing over what happened in school today. We will engage with who we are with and in what we are doing. Mastering our modalities helps us avoid mental frenzy and instead remain present in our current place.

Pillar IV: Meaning

Meaning infuses our lives with purpose and provides us with resilience and satisfaction. We will work to create more meaning in our lives and enhance our wellbeing. Meaning comes from positive relationships and fulfilling activities. It is a powerful tool when other motivators fall short. Meaning blooms when we harness our strengths and when we feel that we bring value to the world and contribute to those around us.

These are the Four Pillars of Thriving, and the following chapters outline how through diligence and resolve we can master Pillar 1. The best versions of us are ready to emerge and thrive, and these four pillars hold the key. Each pillar is its own universe of challenge and opportunity, and we are all capable of mastering their powers.

Pillar I: A Strong Mind

In this book, we begin building powerful defenses to protect our minds and strengthen our resolve. We will learn how to combat distraction and adequately deal with the intrusions that cause pain, suffering, and doubt in our lives. By the end of this book we will know how to deal with stress and fear and use them as fuel.

During our journey through the First Pillar of strengthening our minds, we will work on building our growth mindsets. We will realize that we have the power to achieve our greatest goals and dreams and that we can better ourselves infinitely. We will see that we are surrounded by opportunities to learn, grow, and fix our flaws and faults and make our weaknesses strengths. We will realize that optimism is the most productive and effective outlook, and that difficulties in life are temporary. No matter what we come to face, we will realize that there is not much to fear. We will discover that we have powerful minds, that we are strong and able, and that we can thrive through anything, everything, and beyond.

TOOL #1:
DEALING WITH INTRUSIVE THOUGHTS

The first and fundamental step to building a stronger mind is to deal with intrusive thoughts. If we cannot manage the intrusive thoughts that pop up in our heads and hurt us, we cannot move forward in strengthening ourselves.

Your Mind is a Garden

Imagine the most beautiful garden you have ever seen, filled with fruits, vegetables and flowers of all colors and scents. The garden is healthy, but we recognize that if we do not take care of the garden, it may not stay this way.

One day, a weed starts to grow. Left unattended, the weed begins to flourish and more weeds grow. Over time, weeds start to sprout everywhere and suffocate the garden. Eventually, everything in the neglected garden dies, and nothing new grows. The garden becomes a place littered with decay.

Let's imagine a happier ending. One day, we notice a weed pop up in our beautiful garden. To protect the garden, we pluck the weed immediately. When another weed grows elsewhere in the garden, we pluck that too. Again and again, every time a weed pops its head up, we act quickly to remove it. Over time, after continuously being plucked at their every attempt to rise, the weeds slow in growth and eventually stop intruding on our garden.

Every farmer knows, to create a healthy garden, one must first pluck the weeds and ensure the garden is an environment conducive for growth. After plucking weeds, they will return less frequently and much weaker. This garden is the key to understanding our minds.

When properly taken care of, our minds are healthy and fertile—they flourish and are primed to thrive. When neglected, our minds suffer and deteriorate—negativity begins to breed, and all growth is suffocated. Like the garden, the best way to enrich our minds is to pluck the intrusive thoughts and to plant positive ones. Over time, the intrusive thoughts will quiet down. Eventually, only an occasional pluck will be necessary.

Running from Tigers

The reality is, our minds are wired for survival, not for feeling good. The anxiety we experience in life is what's left of the evolution that helped our distant ancestors escape the hungry saber-toothed tigers that wanted to eat them. While most of us no longer have to worry about getting eaten by giant cats, our fight-or-flight stress response is still operating. This phenomenon is called evolutionary mismatch. It occurs when evolutionary traits once advantageous to us do not adapt appropriately to the changes in our new environment and now work against us.[1] Intrusive thoughts are byproducts of this evolutionary mismatch.

Intrusive Thoughts

Intrusive thoughts are random, automatic thoughts that pop up in our heads and bring us anxiety and suffering. Although intrusive

---

[1] Manus, Melissa B. "Evolutionary Mismatch." *Evolution, Medicine, and Public Health*, Oxford University Press, 8 Aug. 2018, www.ncbi.nlm.nih.gov/pmc/articles/PMC6109377/.

thoughts will definitely persist throughout our lives, we can decide how much power they have over us. There are two types of intrusive thoughts, and identifying them is crucial when deploying the intrusive thought method that we will soon discuss. In short, the intrusive thought method teaches us how to identify both useful and unhelpful thoughts and how to deal with them, respectively. The first types of intrusive thoughts are those that give us valuable information about legitimate dangers. They protect us from harm and encourage corrective actions (like the ones that told your great-great-grandpa to run from the tigers, remember?). The second type of intrusive thoughts involves those that are illusory, petty, mean, or self-deprecating. These types of intrusive thoughts can only bring suffering.

Protection or Suffering?

The intrusive thoughts that only bring suffering are mean, unnecessary thoughts that we don't ask for. They contain hate, cruelty, or unpleasantness, either towards ourselves or to others. These thoughts evoke anger, depression, fear, or doubt—emotions not genuinely representative of our healthiest selves, but rather a side effect of an anxious mind. These types of intrusive thoughts make us question our abilities, our wellbeing, and, at times, even our sanity. Suffering intrusive thoughts like these are tricky because we usually believe them to be true. Many times, we trust them and we think they're real. "You're going to die young," "you're going to lose your job," "your boyfriend broke up with you because you're a terrible person." These are all false intrusive thoughts that bring us pain and suffering. These thoughts are misleading, untrue, and prevent us from feeling good.

As noted above, not all intrusive thoughts are false, and many can be valuable because they are corrective: they are thoughts meant to protect us from harm.

An example may help illustrate this point.

Let's say one morning, a girl named Sophie wakes up and finds a lump on her neck. She feels a bit frightened but concludes that she is sleep deprived and under the weather, so it must be her swollen lymph glands. Sophie moves on with her day. At lunchtime, Sophie unconsciously touches her neck and mistakenly brushes her finger against the lump. She is startled and begins to imagine potential diagnoses. "Could it be a cancerous tumor? Or is it just a cyst?" she thinks.

Sophie tries brushing it off again, telling herself it is only a swollen lymph gland. Weeks pass by, and the lump is still there. Even worse, all that time, Sophie continues having intrusive thoughts that are distracting her from her day. She keeps trying to dismiss the thoughts, but they keep coming back to haunt her. The reason: the thought is corrective and is trying to encourage her to take corrective action.

In Sophie's case, corrective action is booking a doctor's appointment to confirm that the lump isn't anything serious. Until a doctor checks the lump, Sophie will not have mental peace. The intrusive thought is the mind's way of telling Sophie, "Get the lump checked! See what it is!" The thoughts here are corrective and are trying to protect Sophie.

The Intrusive Thought Method: For Suffering Thoughts

When an intrusive thought pops up, determine whether the thought is a corrective one or not. If it addresses a real problem and offers you a means of resolving that problem, then it is corrective. If it does not address a real problem or fails to provide any path to resolution, then it can only bring worry.

Deep down, we all know in our core whether a thought is truly real or is us simply psyching ourselves out. While it may not seem obvious to you all the time, when we look deeply into ourselves, emotions and panic aside, we know if we truly need to concern ourselves with a thought.

If you determine the intrusive thought is causing you false suffering rather than warning you for valid protection, dismiss the thought and don't deal with it. Dismissing a thought does not mean ignoring or disregarding the thought. Dismissing a thought means letting it stay and not giving it power. It's looking at the thought, acknowledging its existence, and invalidating it by not giving it attention. Sit with the thought. Let it sit within you. Feel what you feel. Disempower the thought by moving forward with your life regardless. The alternative, such as debating the thought or trying to push it away, gives it energy and any engagement with it feeds its power and makes it more real to you. When you let the thought stay regardless, it disappears faster and faster. The more you let it stay and drift on its own, the less it comes back. When it does come back, just repeat.

Although a thought that only brings suffering occasionally protects us from harm, the vast majority of these worrisome thoughts are false and can be dismissed. These are usually sudden and reactionary ideas that bring feelings of self-doubt, resentment, and fear. These thoughts come from our reptilian brain, which is the oldest part of our heads wired for survival.

Our reptilian brain includes the structures that populate most of a reptile's brain, the brainstem and cerebellum, responsible for important functions like heart rate, breathing, and body temperature. Although valuable, our reptilian brain could become stubborn and obsessive.[2]

Because this anatomy is in control of our instinctive self-preserving behavior when we feel overwhelmed or stressed, the

---

[2] "The Evolutionary Layers of the Human Brain." *The Brain from Top to Bottom*, McGill, thebrain.mcgill.ca/flash/d/d_05/d_05_cr/d_05_cr_her/d_05_cr_her.html.

reptilian brain activates under stress. Many times, we forget that this "croc" brain is separate from us and that its thoughts are not truly us. However, these thoughts will continue nagging at us until we deal with them properly.

The Mental Fire Alarm

Most people struggle to dismiss the intrusive thoughts that bring them suffering because they trust these thoughts too much and spend a great deal of their time considering their implications. Many struggle because they believe the suffering thoughts attacking them are anything but arbitrary or illusory. They listen to these negative thoughts that beat them down by telling them they're pathetic, weak, or wicked. They ruminate on these thoughts and give them credibility, saying, "Maybe there's truth here that I need to consider for the future." The truth is these thoughts are just false claims. They are uninvited and triggered during the natural roller coaster of life.

Most people have experienced how startling a fire alarm blast can be. When it goes off, it throws the entire home into panic and quickly springs everyone into action. Thankfully, a vast majority of the time, there is no actual danger or fire—it is just a false alarm. The culprits usually include smoke from cooking food, steam from showers, and debris on sensors. The only problem is fire departments respond to false alarms as if there were actual danger. In 2012, U.S. fire departments responded to 2,238,000 false alarms, 713,000 of which were caused by system malfunctions.[3]

Similarly, we all tend to respond to these "false alarm" thoughts in our minds. Although our suffering thoughts originally intended

[3] Ahrens, Marty. "NFPA's 'Smoke Alarms in U.S. Home Fires.'" *News & Research*, National Fire Protection Association, Jan. 2019, www.nfpa.org/News-and-Research/ Data-research-and-tools/Emergency-Responders/False-alarm-activity-in-the-US.

to protect us from harm, our many hurtful thoughts today should be thought of as false alarms caused by system malfunctions that should be dismissed. Most home fire deaths do not occur because an alarm goes off and people fail to respond correctly. Most fire deaths happen from fires in homes that don't have smoke alarms or have broken ones. Since we know our fight-or-flight system is installed, our primary focus should be how to appropriately respond to the alarms, true or false, that go off.

The Intrusive Thought Method: For Corrective Thoughts

As alluded to above, there is a difference between dismissing a false alarm and disregarding an alarm that may have truth. Disregarding a fire alarm altogether is foolish and dangerous. If a fire alarm goes off, it is irresponsible to assume everything is okay and that there is no fire. Similarly, we should not walk around life blindly, ignoring the warning signs found in our thoughts.

Take a chronic cigarette smoker experiencing terrible lung and throat irritation. If the smoker experiences intrusive thoughts about contracting cancer, it is neither healthy nor intelligent for the smoker to assume that there are no real problems or that ignoring the uncomfortable thoughts is the solution. It is, in fact, likely that the intrusive thoughts are corrective. Therefore, in this case, disregarding and not acknowledging the fire alarm is irresponsible.

Only after acknowledging the alarm and proving it to be false, or identifying it to be accurate and taking corrective action, can one dismiss the thoughts. In the case of the cigarette smoker, the mind is indeed sending anxiety-provoking thoughts as warning signs to protect the individual. These are corrective intrusive thoughts. In cases like these, where we identify that the thought is warning us about something valid, we must take corrective action to quiet the mind. It is up to the person to do what is right for himself. The cigarette smoker could choose to use the intrusive thought method to eliminate these corrective thoughts, and eventually, the thoughts will go away. What is dangerous, however, is the cigarette smoker would then be without a figurative fire alarm and at risk of actually facing a fire—smoking until he contracts cancer. The correct way to eliminate intrusive thoughts encouraging corrective action is to take the corrective action the thoughts recommend, not to ignore them.

Once corrective action is taken, if the thoughts continue to return, we could then responsibly label them as intrusive and dismiss them since we are already on the case. Going back to our example with Sophie and the lump on her neck, once Sophie books the doctor's appointment, corrective action has been taken. Therefore, any intrusive thoughts that arise after this point are no longer of service to Sophie, and she should dismiss them. She is already on the case. The intrusive thoughts are no longer providing her valid protection. The thoughts are only causing unnecessary fear and anxiety about a problem for which Sophie has already taken corrective action.

The fire alarm analogy works here as well. Let's say a fire alarm rings in David's home. After identifying a real problem, David calls the fire department, and they arrive shortly after. The head fireman comes to David after assessing the situation and says that they are aware of the issue and are working on it. The fireman also warns David that the alarm may keep ringing from time to time, but they are in the house and on the case, so he has no reason to worry. It is undeniable that David now has no reason to be concerned when the alarm goes off again. David should not panic nor stew in thought as he already took corrective action, and everything that could be done is being done to solve the problem.

The same is true for us. If we decide our thoughts are indeed warning us about real concerns in our lives, we must determine whether we are taking the proper corrective action being asked of us. If we conclude that we are doing everything we currently can to address the issue, we should dismiss the thought as it is no longer of service to us.

How Do We Know For Sure?

While the intrusive thought method above is fine and dandy, some people struggle more than others with suffering intrusive thoughts. Some people deal with these abusive, automatic thoughts daily, making them question themselves and their judgment. How could they know for sure that their thoughts telling them they are terrible or insufficient are intrusive and should be dismissed? What if those thoughts are true and real and should be kept and analyzed? What if their corrective action is not enough and there are serious issues at hand? The best way to answer this question is to look at hoarders.

Hoarding

Hoarders are people who excessively save worthless items to their detriment. They cannot part with their possessions, and the clutter ultimately disrupts their lives. Most of the time, a hoarder's excuse for saving an item is that it will be valuable in the future. While we understand that the individual will likely not need most of the items they are hoarding, hoarders have a pretty strong rationale for holding unto their belongings:[4]

> "Why do you need this flower vase that has been sitting here for five years?"

---

[4] *What Is Hoarding Disorder?* American Psychiatric Association, www.psychiatry.org/patients-families/hoarding-disorder/what-is-hoarding-disorder.

"Well, someone may buy me flowers, so I am going to need it."

"Okay, but why do you need three of them? Can't you just save one?"

"Well, one of them may break and so then I will need the others. Plus, the flowers may be different sizes and require different vases."

Many times, hoarders are deeply afraid that they will one day need the items they are saving, and if they were to give it away, it would be problematic to them.

"Can we throw out all these old newspapers?"

"Absolutely not, I need them."

"Why? They are from over five years ago."

"Well, there are interesting articles. A family member or I may need to reference one. Look at this: How to treat cancer naturally. The cure for cancer is sitting right here and you want me to throw it out."

"Okay, but can't you do your research if the time comes when you need to? The article also looks like it may be outdated..."

"I cannot throw them out. They are very important and I want them at arm's reach so I can access them quickly if needed."

It is highly likely that the item being hoarded by the hoarder is unnecessary and could be tossed—like the false alarms mentioned above. If the hoarder needed the vase, he'd be using it.

The only way for the hoarder to heal is for him to realize that he will be okay without the item being hoarded. Therefore, the first step is for a hoarder to take a risk and throw out the item.

Psychology professionals believe that the most effective way to overcome a fear is to voluntarily encounter the fear and confront it. When dealing with fear, the goal is not to become less afraid, but to become braver when facing fears.

The same applies to our intrusive thoughts that bring suffering. While everyone has a part of themselves that may want to believe that most of our suffering thoughts are real, hold power, and symbolize truth, we must take the risk of dismissing them and see if they stand. Like hoarders, too many of us obsessively save worthless views to our detriment. We cannot part from the automatic thoughts that pop up and clutter and disrupt our minds. Similar to hoarders, we feel these beliefs hold weight and reflect consequences for the future. It's an exhausting conflict deciding whether or not we should trust and keep certain thoughts. Therefore, we must take a risk and jump. Most of the time, intrusive thoughts that attack our being could be thrown out. Over time, as we work the muscle of dismissing these intruders, we will get better at it.

Hoarders need to take a risk and de-clutter to make room for living space. In the same way, we must take the risk of dismissing suffering thoughts that may have truth to make room for a clear mind and for living healthily in the present. The hoarder will die faster from something brought in by hoarding rather than from giving up that which they hoard. The same is true for your suffering intrusive thoughts, obsessive worries, and mental clutter; they will destroy aspects of your life before that which you fear does. It is worth taking the risk to dismiss one suffering thought that provides real concern out of 10,000 suffering thoughts that are valueless to live a beautiful life, rather than have all those suffering thoughts and live a life of struggle.

TOOL #2:
TURNING OPTIMISM INTO A MINDSET

Our mindset affects the way we experience the outside world and the way we live our lives. It is the lens through which we take in the events around us and develop the beliefs within us.

What We Have in Common with Baby Elephants

When a trainer begins training a baby elephant, she ties a rope around one of the elephant's legs and attaches it to a post. The elephant fights for hours and, ultimately, days, attempting to escape the line. After endless failed attempts to pull free, the elephant realizes it will not win, so it gives up, settles down, and accepts its range of motion.

Eventually, the elephant grows into a massive adult, strong enough to easily break free from the trainer's leash. However, the elephant doesn't even try. Once the elephant has accepted that trying to escape is useless, it gives up and no longer attempts to break free. This phenomenon is known as learned helplessness.[5]

We are not so different from baby elephants. We go through life encountering a lot of tough times and painfully discover that we may need more work on ourselves than we had initially hoped.

---

[5] "Learned Helplessness." *Finding Meaning: The Sixth Stage of Grief*, by David Kessler, Scribner, 2020, pp. 87–88.

Over time, the events in our lives influence our perspectives, rein-forcing the belief systems that determine how we look at our obstacles and our abilities to overcome them.

Pessimism and Optimism

Pessimism is the tendency to see the worst in things and to have a lack of hope for the future. Many of us may believe that our struggles and shortcomings are permanent. Each of us says things like, "I never have good luck," when we buy a losing lot-tery ticket, or "This is who I am," when we can't improve our habits, or "This always happens to me," when we catch a flat tire. We may also believe that the bad things that happen are pervasive and will affect our entire lives. We say things like, "This is going to kill me," when we struggle on diets, or "I'm losing everything," when we are let go from a job, or "I'm bad at math," when we fail an exam. We also take things personally, blaming ourselves for bad events and crediting only good events to external forces. All in all, these ways of thinking are pessimistic, making our future seem bleak, where the worst will happen.

Our goal is to have more optimism in our lives. We want to feel hopeful and confident about ourselves and the future. Here, we recognize struggles are inevitable and temporary, that setbacks are related to short-term circumstances that we have the power to influence. Optimists say things like, "Work has been challeng-ing lately, but all will be okay," or "I did not prepare properly for my basketball game, so I did terribly. I will practice and do better next time." We do not take suffering personally and recognize that it is inevitable in life. We acknowledge we have to improve our health and pursue more worthwhile or fruitful habits. We under-stand we are not as great as we could be, but it is okay because we will work on our shortcomings and treat each day as a chance to better ourselves. As optimists, we isolate troubling events and compartmentalize them away from the rest of our lives. We generally believe that good things are coming.

It is important to note that data shows those with more optimism usually have stronger immune systems, more meaningful relationships, and generally more successful lives.[6]

Either way, no matter which of the perspectives we relate to more, we possess both of them, and we need both optimism and pessimism to navigate life successfully. Too much optimism could lead to overconfidence bias (ever hear of Titanic?)[7], and not enough pessimism could dwindle our belief that we need to prepare for challenges. On the other hand, too little optimism and too much pessimism could lead us to never challenge our limitations or pursue new interests out of a belief that we are destined to fail. Each of us is on the spectrum between the two, and it is our goal to find the healthiest balance for ourselves.

Internal Dialogue

When your mind goes blank during a presentation, what do you tell yourself? Do you say that you are terrible at public speaking, that you will never have charisma no matter what you do, that you will never grow your skillset? Or, do you tell yourself that this specific presentation was challenging and that you will prepare

---

[6] Gillham, Jane E, et al. "Optimism, Pessimism, and Explanatory Style." *Optimism and Pessimism: Implications for Theory, Research, and Practice*, by Edward C. Chang, American Psychological Association, 2001, pp. 53–75.

[7] "We place absolute confidence in the Titanic. We believe the boat is unsinkable!" -P.A.S. Franklin, V.P. White Star Line. Root. "Why Did People Consider the Titanic Unsinkable?" History, History, 15 May 2018, www.historyonthenet.com/the-titanic-why-did-people-believe-titanic-was-unsinkable.

better next time? Do you tell yourself that public speaking is a skill that needs practice and that you will get better in time?

When a recruiter rejects you for a position at your dream company, do you believe it is because you're unintelligent? Do you believe that everyone feels that way about you and that you'll never have a successful career? Or do you recognize that this one person may have her reasons for not recruiting you, but that you are still a fantastic person with many options to succeed?

These are all examples of internal dialogue. This dialogue happens automatically, and when you find yourself feeling a certain way about yourself or others, it is your internal dialogue that is running. Unfortunately, many people have pessimistic internal dialogues, and they don't even know that they could change them. Most people don't realize that they can direct their internal dialogue to help them rather than hurt them. Each time you listen to and accept negative internal messaging, you are reinforcing it and making the irrational belief stronger.

Here are more examples of pessimistic internal dialogue:

- Those people are much better than me.
- I didn't perform well in my job; my boss is going to fire me.
- Why couldn't I do that; I am just not good at anything.
- Nobody is interested in talking to me.
- I am so clumsy. That's why this happened.
- I can't get people to be my friend.
- I am a failure. Look at me.
- See, I can't solve this problem.

It seems as though the internal dialogue happens all by itself. But where does this pessimistic self-talk come from?

Here are some possibilities, although the origin of the negative internal dialogue doesn't matter so much as the way to get rid of it:

- Thinking traps.
- Baseless thoughts about yourself and the world.
- Moodiness that causes a negative mindset.
- Being highly critical about yourself.
- Holding onto negative past experiences and worrying that they will repeat themselves.

Events in Life Are Not Personal

The first step to overcoming this crippling kind of negativity is recognizing that life events aren't personal. When your friend does not answer your text, it does not automatically mean she is ignoring you because she is upset with you. It could be that she had a busy day and couldn't get to your message. When your family member is stricken with an illness, it isn't because he is your relative and there is some curse forcing you to inevitably deal with hardship all your life. Everyone deals with hardship, and whoever hasn't yet, will.

When feeling personally attacked, whether by others or by life itself, you must remind yourself that you aren't alone suffering in a world out to get you. Life is challenging to all, and even attacks on you personally could be due to circumstances that ultimately have nothing to do with you. For example, your boss may have yelled at you at the office one day not because she doesn't like you or was upset with your job performance, but because she was having problems at home, or was having a tough day and could not adequately express her specific concerns with you in a constructive manner. You may have contracted the flu before an exciting trip not because your luck would have it that way but because you spent the week before cramming for finals, not eating well, and barely sleeping. Illness sometimes just happens when you are stressed and exhausted.

We must remember that life is not personal. While things may seem to be happening to us, they are not. They are merely happening around us. We encounter them and respond as farers on our journeys of life.

Events in Life Are Not Permanent

When you encounter a struggle or a setback, it is crucial to understand that the obstacle at hand is temporary, not permanent. Even when something permanent happens, like losing a loved one, the suffering and sadness are temporary. Each one of us will emerge from the experience and move forward from the pain. If we do not, we cannot thrive.

It is a Buddhist understanding that the temporariness of life is what makes it so unique and beautiful.[8] Flowers are precious because they are temporary and fragile. A shooting star is magical because of how quickly it forms, inspires, and then disappears. A sunset is breathtaking because its beauty is ever-changing, each second, a color is evolving slightly, a shadow shifting subtly, making each passing moment a single independent experience.

The above is also true with the hardships of life. Although very painful, the trials and tribulations we encounter are temporary and vary in length. Our duty as individuals is to first accept this truth and then thrive alongside with it.

Events in Life Are Not Pervasive

The way you look at your weaknesses, interpret criticism and respond to rejection all have a significant effect on your ability to thrive.

---

8 Hanh Nhất, and Melvin McLeod. *The Pocket Thich Nhất Hanh*. Shambhala Publications, Inc., 2017.

If you struggle with math or are deficient in vocabulary, you are not unintelligent, but rather weaker in those specific areas and must work on them.

When your friend tells you that you're a selfish or arrogant person, it is not that you are a selfish or arrogant human being with nothing else to you. The criticism does not reflect your overall identity. His criticism is just revealing that he feels you are acting selfishly and behaving arrogantly but this specific conduct is not representative of your best self.

When you are rejected from a job, a university, or a date, you are not being turned down because you are insufficient as a person. While in some situations it may be appropriate to blame yourself or others for rejection, many times rejections occur simply because of mismatch. Sometimes the fit is not right.[9]

A company may value certain qualities and qualifications when they are searching for candidates, and these criteria may not align with the attributes you have and value for yourself. They may value a college degree and a willingness to work long hours more than the work experience and balanced life you value. In cases like these, their metrics of assessment simply don't match your profile because you valued other things throughout your life that influenced the decisions you made, and these decisions ultimately affected what landed on your resume.

In high school, you may have decided to trade off having a 4.0 GPA and perfect SAT score to participate in extracurricular activities and hobbies you enjoy, like join a sports team or school club, and spend meaningful time with your family and friends. Because this decision brought you wellbeing in the areas of life that were most important to you, there is no disappointment in

---

[9] TED. "Bouncing Back from Rejection, *Work Life with Adam Grant,* Season 2, Episode 7, Apple Podcasts p. 16, Apr. 2019.

being rejected from a university that places most of its value in a candidate's GPA and SAT, and not on an individual's success in other areas of life like in engaging hobbies, meaningful activities, and healthy and positive relationships.

A person may reject you if you ask them on a date because they value financial standing or certain physical attributes more than they value character and personality in the people they date. They didn't reject you because you're an ugly, horrible person with no potential for love who will forever live alone. It is because the match wasn't there. The fit wasn't right.

We must remember that the problems in our lives are not pervasive and all-encompassing. In almost all cases, a problem's influence does not extend beyond a single sphere of our lives. When we encounter financial struggles, our whole lives should not come crumbling down into chaos. We still have our health, our relationships, and our wellbeing in other areas. If we release a poem or piece of music that critics completely hate, the "terrible" work does not represent who we are. The criticism is just an opinion from one specific audience on one particular sample of work that we produced and shared. We simply now have important feedback and know precise ways in which we can improve.

Either way, there is way more to us than the glimpses that most people see. We may have moments where we behave as bad friends, but we may also be great sons, daughters, brothers, sisters, aunts, and uncles. We may have an exam where we do not perform well but then perform exceptionally well on the basketball court during an important game. Events in life are not pervasive, there is a lot to us.

Beware of Thinking Traps

It is important to note that when we confront difficult moments in life, we are prone to fall into thinking traps—certain types or patterns of pessimistic thoughts that trap us in anxiety and do not allow productive proactive progress.[10] We must learn to acknowledge and identify our most common thinking traps because they disguise themselves subtly in our daily thoughts and negatively influence our internal dialogue. Using deliberate effort, we must spot the thinking traps that hurt us most and overcome them individually rather than fall prey to them. On the following page, we will explore the most common thinking traps we encounter and examples of the pessimistic internal dialogue they trigger: [11]

Thinking Traps	Examples
Fortune-telling: Predicting negative things about the future.	*"I know I'm going to fail."* *"I will never be able to succeed."*
Black-and-white thinking: Looking at situations in extremes (i.e., good or bad, right or wrong, success or failure).	*"Anything below an A is a failure."* *"I ate a cookie, now my entire diet is ruined!"*
Mind-reading: Believing we know what others are thinking and assuming the worst.	*"She thinks I'm dumb."* *"They don't like me."*
Over-generalization: Describing situations in absolutes, using words like "always" or "never".	*"I always mess up."* *"I will never be good at math."*
Labeling: Using overarchingly mean or negative words to describe ourselves.	*"I'm weak."* *"I'm pathetic."*

[10] "Thinking Traps." *Thinking Traps | Anxiety Canada Youth*, youth.anxietycanada.com/thinking-traps.

[11] "Thinking Traps." *Thinking Traps | Anxiety Canada*, www.anxietycanada.com/sites/default/files/ThinkingTraps.pdf.

Questioning Pessimistic Perspective

Our internal dialogues have pessimistic tendencies when we encounter uncomfortable or undesired events in life. However, these first impressions are not always accurate. Therefore, we must not believe the messages until there is concrete evidence for them. We must remember, simply because we are thinking a certain thought, it does not mean the thought is true. Many times, our internal dialogue is falling prey to thinking traps. Think, for example, we are sitting in our favorite restaurant and a waiter that is usually friendly to us walks past without saying hello. We are tempted to conclude that the waiter is being rude and is ignoring us on purpose. However, we should properly question our belief by asking, "Is there any proof to support our assumption?" There are many factors that could have caused the waiter to ignore us. Maybe he is in a sour mood after hearing bad news, and his behavior has nothing to do with us at all!

Actively State Positive Messages to Yourself. And Prove It!

Our internal dialogues are not very creative. Once they have become comfortable with a message, they will repeat it over and over again. When these messages spite, they are at worst a nuisance, but they can become serious burdens when they are negative and uncontrolled.

Ruminating on these negative messages will do us no good. Instead, we must talk back to the inner critic and reject its claims. If, for example, our internal dialogues insult us and accuse us of being failures, then we need to embrace the opposite and say, 'I am successful.' We could then find proof in our lives for successes no matter how insignificant they are or even start taking action in areas we know need improving now. Either way, we must not just accept the critic in our heads. We must dismiss the voice telling us we are failures. We must speak proudly of our successes and triumphs. We must focus on our present and past achievements while taking steps to realize the accomplishments we seek in the future.

Two Mindsets

Generally, our beliefs fall under two mindset categories: growth mindset and fixed mindset. Many people tend to default to a fixed mindset, believing they have a certain intelligence and ability level that they cannot change or influence. Those with fixed mindsets believe their minds are static. They avoid challenges outside of their comfort zones, ignore useful criticism, and feel threatened by the success of others. People with fixed mindsets also tend to give up easily, seeing effort as fruitless. Generally, those with fixed mindsets take less risk and, in turn, set lower goals. Unfortunately, there is a lot of potential (and wellbeing) lost here.

Fortunately for fixed mindsets (and everyone else), science has discovered the concept of neuroplasticity – the idea that human brains could change form and physiologically strengthen in synaptic connections over our lives from experience and learning.

The science behind neuroplasticity is simple. Our brains can form new neural connections either in response to injury or to adjust to new situations by growing new nerve endings that reconnect to broken neurons responsible for vital functions.[12]

Lucky for us, we can take advantage of this ability. Because our brains are equipped to do so, we can strengthen ourselves in areas we choose, including our minds. We can become smarter,

---

[12] Jr., William C. Shiel. "Medical Definition of Neuroplasticity." *MedicineNet*, MedicineNet, 24 Jan. 2017, www.medicinenet.com/script/main/art.asp?articlekey=40362.

better, and faster with deliberate practice (more on this later). Whether in mental health, football, or cooking, our minds are malleable and can be developed and cultivated through effort. This brings us to the growth mindset.

Growth mindset is the belief (and the scientific reality) that we and our minds are malleable and can advance through learning and practice.[13] This means our personalities are malleable, and we are not stuck being the way we currently are. Our habits are malleable, so we can learn to rewire our patterns and our behaviors. Our perspectives are malleable, so we can alter our beliefs and our values. Our intelligence is malleable, so we are not limited by our IQs or our perceived "weaknesses." Understanding this truth is critical in moving forward in our lives. We must understand the indisputable fact that we can change and absolutely *can* grow in areas we desire. It is a scientifically proven fact that we are not stuck in the areas where we are unhappy.

We each have growth and fixed mindsets in different areas of our lives. You may have a growth mindset when it comes to sports because you believe you could learn and master a new sport with some practice, but have a fixed mindset toward academics because you feel like you're terrible at math and reinforce this belief by refusing to try to improve. The result from these mindsets is that you quickly (and happily) learn new sports but have no progress in math.

Our goal as people should be to cultivate our growth mindset in as many areas of life as possible. Why? Because neuroplasticity is proven! Neuroplasticity has even been used to heal people from chronic illness and agonizing symptoms.[14]

---

[13] Holmes, Nigel, and Carol S. Dweck. *Two Mindsets*
[14] Doidge, Norman. *The Brain That Changes Itself: Stories of Personal Triumph from the Frontiers of Brain Science*. London: Penguin, 2007. Print.

Science proves we could be better, so why wouldn't we believe it?

Stop the Trash Talk

Stop asking yourself why you are the way you are. Stop mourning your weak mindset, your terrible habits, and the areas in life you wish you were better. You can change! Focus on change. Stop telling yourself that you're too afraid, or unqualified, or too late to do something. That's utter nonsense. What science could guarantee is that your consistent trash talk against yourself is convincing your brain that you are afraid, weak, and hopeless. Free yourself from your lies!

You Can

Tell yourself you can. Realize and reinforce the belief that you have what it takes to do whatever you put your mind to with time and practice. You can change for the better in any area you choose. You just need the right tools and strategies to do so.

Learning to ride a bike is an excellent parallel. No one is born knowing how to ride a bike. However, if you put in the time and the practice to learn some technique and develop your abilities, you will eventually get to the point that you can take off your training wheels and ride on your own. You will undoubtedly fall and tumble, and even get scratched and scream like bloody hell. This is without a doubt. However, you will be gliding along with smiles soon enough.

Life is the same. It may take longer and hurt a bit more, but you are capable and far stronger than you think. You just need to realize that you are. You are equipped with the most magnificent instrument in the universe, your mind, and you just need the tools and strategies to optimize your mindset for the journey. You need to learn to ride the bike.

You will be scared, but fear is okay. Feel the fear and move forward anyway. Give yourself a bit of credit, some room for failure, and take the first courageous step. It will be okay. Just start shutting down the trash-talking and turning up the encouragement. All your hopes and dreams are waiting for you. Free yourself from your prison.

TOOL #3:
DEALING WITH FEELINGS

As human beings, we are continually experiencing feelings that form the fabric of our life experience. Fun moments, like spending quality time with our friends at a nice restaurant, give us feelings of love and joy. Exciting moments, like an anticipated first date or the first day of school, bring us thrill and delight. These special moments fuel us, and our senses radiate from these experiences.

Feelings are called feelings because we *feel* them. Science has shown that feelings bring us physical sensations and that they are experienced throughout our bodies. We have all felt the warmth of a real hug, the stomach-tickling hilarity of a funny joke, and the genuine sweetness in a baby's laugh. It is in our nature to feel these pleasures. As human beings, we feel and enjoy positive emotions. We are naturally pulled towards them. [15]

As we all know too well, life reveals difficult moments to us as well—moments that can be quite painful and sad and can bring us uncomfortable feelings. We have all felt knots in our stomachs from bad news, like a phone call from a brother informing us that our grandfather passed away earlier that day. We have all felt

---

[15] Nummenmaa, Lauri, et al. "Bodily Maps of Emotions." *PNAS*, National Academy of Sciences, 14 Jan. 2014, www.pnas.org/content/111/2/646.

the hard lump in our throat after our first love says things need to end. We have all felt the sour anxiety and chilling hopelessness that comes with losing a job or having a health scare. These moments hurt, and they leave us feeling alone and frightened. We feel that we are stuck, that we are insufficient and insignificant. We become overwhelmed with feelings that we cannot take on the burdensome challenges and responsibilities inevitable in this life. We feel insecure and afraid. We dread embarrassing ourselves and falling flat in front of our family and friends who are all watching and seem to be doing better than we are.

Whether positive or negative, we all "feel" across the emotional spectrum every day. We oscillate daily from things happening around us, to us, and within us, and each trigger emotions within us. Some days we wake up happy and motivated by default. On others, we are complacent and gloomy. There are even days where we start off feeling good and excited, but by midday, we're irritated and pessimistic, or vice versa. Our feelings are exactly like the weather, changing from day to day and throughout each day. It could be sunny today and rainy tomorrow, clear now and cloudy later. Regardless of our feelings, however, we shouldn't lead our lives differently.

Our Internal Weather

When we wake up in the morning with an important agenda for the day, the weather never stops us from doing what we set out to accomplish. The weather may make tasks more difficult for us, but very rarely do we let the weather get in the way of our plans. There would have to be a severe heatwave or a snowy blizzard outside for us to sit home idly all day despite having scheduled a busy and productive day for ourselves.

Our relationship with our feelings must be the same way. In the same way that the world continues to operate regardless of weather, we should keep thriving in our lives irrespective of our feelings. We must take on our days' agendas and set out to accomplish what we intended to do even when we do not feel our best.

Isolate Feelings from Identity

These days we often identify ourselves with our feelings. We say, "I am angry," or "I am hurt," rather than, "I am feeling angry," or "I feel hurt." What is unfortunate about identifying ourselves with our feelings is that it places our decisions and behavior at the whim of external forces and events that fluctuate uncontrollably in our lives. We will inevitably encounter difficulty and discomfort, and our feelings will develop directly from our experiences with them. Therefore, we must learn to manage our feelings or, at the very least, detach ourselves from them so that we remain in control of our lives. We need to be more than we feel!

If we were to wake up on the day of a significant event—say, an important class presentation, a big job interview, or a playoff basketball game—and stub our pinky toe hard on the leg of the bed frame, it is very likely we will be overwhelmed by the pain, swear angrily for an instant, and then move on with our day to do what we need to do. Odds are, we will succeed in our day despite the irritating wakeup and forget about the broken toenail.

We must act the same way toward our feelings. Our sad spirits, bad moods, and angry attitudes are just stubbed pinky toes that must be felt and moved on from so that we can achieve what we set out to do. What is real transcends what we feel.

Influencing Feelings

There are many instances in life where our feelings are too powerful to be overcome through only isolating them. We feel butterflies in our stomachs, pain in our tightening backs, and lumps in our throats. When we can't seem to separate the feelings away from our physical beings and daily experience, we must employ more powerful strategies.

Physiology

Scientific studies confirm that the way we pose—our body language—directly influences how we feel, think, and behave. When we stand in high-power poses – which is common when we are behaving with confidence or bravery in times of excitement, our hormone levels change and make us better versions of ourselves. In men, testosterone levels increase, which gives a greater sense of confidence and self-esteem, and there is a decrease in cortisol levels, the hormone responsible for the stress we experience. The data shows that posing as our most confident selves, even artificially, brings us psychological, physiological, and behavioral transformations that help us elevate our wellbeing, effectively deal with stress, make better decisions, and think more clearly.[16]

When we feel like we are weak and subjugated by our feelings, we must ask, how would the most confident versions of ourselves stand? How would the strongest versions of ourselves breathe and walk? What would we look like if we were in a place of clarity? We must put ourselves in a physical position that matches the way we want to feel—the way we would stand, move, and behave if we were thriving. We should stand up straight, broaden our shoulders, and stick our chests out because that is what the best versions of ourselves would do.

---

[16] Cuddy, Amy. "Your Body Language May Shape Who You Are." TED, www.ted.com/talks/amy_cuddy_your_body_language_may_shape_who_you_are/up-next?language=en

Focus

Although the physiology method is tried and true, our minds will still try to battle us and divert our attention to what is bothering us. Therefore, we must work on our focus.

Focus is powerful in that it determines what we will believe and how we feel throughout our days. If we look closely at any-thing—a decision, a person, or an idea—and search for problems with them, we will find them. There is hard evidence for every-thing. The reality is that things are not meant to be perfect. It is quite the opposite. The natural state of things is chaos, and we must find and create order in our experience. The natural state is not a world of perfection, where chaos suddenly shows up and ruins things. Chaos innately exists, and order must be created to make things great.

If we focus on what is wrong and missing, we will feel and see what is wrong and missing. If we focus on what is right and what is good, we will feel and see what is right and good. The way we change our focus is through changing the questions we subcon-sciously ask ourselves.

Subconscious questions direct all our thoughts. Every time we ask a question to ourselves or others ask us a question, we are forced to think and find an answer in our minds.

- What color is the sky?
- What did you have for breakfast today?
- What was the worst day of your life?
- What was the saddest moment you had this year?
- What is your favorite ice cream?
- What is your greatest memory?

All these questions make you think. They make you recall the memories and information you have stored in your mind because for every question, you must ponder an answer. Therefore, change your focus by asking yourself better questions.

"What are my options right now?" is a better question than, "What disaster is likely to come from the problem I am facing right now?" Other, more productive questions include:

- What are the possible solutions to my problem?
- What are the productive steps I could take to handle this issue better?
- How can I improve this situation?
- What would the best version of myself do in this scenario?
- How would someone I admire deal with this challenge?

These new, more constructive questions force our minds to focus on positive and useful answers available to us rather than on painful, intimidating difficulties we fear. Focusing on the issue at hand would only bring us discomfort at best and debilitating fear at worst. If we focus on a wall while driving, we will drive right into the wall. Alternatively, refocusing towards helpful thoughts brings us value and guides us towards progress. We must focus on what we want and on the solutions that exist to help us. We live in a world where too many things demand our attention, and if we don't choose what to focus on, then the world will steal our attention and decide for us. It is time to take our focus back.

Language

The way we speak dramatically affects how we feel and who we become. Coming home from work, saying, "I feel so terrible, I'm exhausted, and I had the longest day," produces a different experience than when we say, "I am so tired, what an action-packed day I had! I am so happy I get to relax and unwind now." Productive, successful people preserve their energy and their moods by speaking constructively. Rather than feeling "beat" after a busy day, they feel accomplished and fulfilled because that is the story they tell using their language. Weak and struggling people do the opposite, hurting their attitudes and spirits by speaking destructively.

When we feel fatigued and world-weary, we should concentrate on the way we speak and enhance our language. Over time, if we consciously complain less and use less negative talk, we will feel better and live more productively. If we remain mindful when speaking and put effort into using more positive language, the tendency will automate itself, and we will feel better in our lives.

An effective way to utilize the power of our language is by employing specificity. Many times, we feel overwhelmed and overtaken by our issues because we perceive our whole world to be crashing down upon us when we're faced with serious struggle. Specificity allows us to focus on what exactly our challenge is and how we could move towards triumphing over it. We must precisely identify the particular thing that is troubling us, and then devise a means of fixing it. If we do not hone in on the problem and fix it, we stand susceptible to the consuming anxiety that everything is wrong, which leaves us feeling helpless. Instead of saying, "I am a failure in school," say, "I am underperforming in math." Language can be used to make the emotions that we're feeling either larger or smaller. Instead of saying, "I'm depressed," say, "I feel depressed about this specific problem." Instead of saying,

"I'm unhappy in my relationship," say, "I feel upset about this specific element in my relationship." No one is generally upset about everything; it is usually only one thing that we're scared to confront.

Beliefs

Many times, our feelings are influenced by the beliefs we hold about ourselves and the world around us. Sometimes these beliefs bring us great pain because we worry about things that are either outside our control entirely or beyond our influence at the time and, therefore, beyond our immediate control. We must make an effort to question the assumptions we make in our minds. We must find comfort in the parts of life we do not have power over and the realities that we must accept at the moment.

Falling Short

There are many times in life where we expect to reach a milestone and do not. There are those of us who are beyond the age that we expected to be married and are "still" single. Some of us expected to have active careers by now but are "still" stuck where we are. Others had hoped to have a child by now, but no child is in sight. Regardless of our beliefs and expectations, there is a relatable pain we all feel when we believe we have "fallen short."

We may try to convince ourselves that everything will work out or that everything is for the best. Sometimes we think, "I have to strengthen my faith in God." Regardless, we are still in pain from these feelings because we didn't achieve what we believed we were supposed to.

Another weak coping method we use is to smother these feelings by rationalizing that "other people have it worse than me." That may be true, but it does very little to quiet these ill feelings. When we feel frustrated after failing to meet our goals, we are in states of quiet desperation. We look around, and all we can see are people who seem to have what we're lacking. Those people seem to be following us wherever we go, exacerbating our suffering.

Desired Outcomes

Our distress in situations like these is generally caused by our latching to specific results. When the specific result does not unfold the way we hope, we become upset. This is a natural way to feel. Nonetheless, the underlying outcomes we have become attached to come from arbitrary desires. The outcomes we envision are simply some of the many ways in which we can fulfill our underlying needs. A goal of improved health, for example, may not mean losing 10 pounds in a month. It may mean starting with one juice per day or taking a 20-minute walk each morning.

Stop Forcing Reality

To combat frustration, we must let go of what we believe reality should be. We stay frustrated because we are stuck over what we (falsely) believe reality should be:

- There shouldn't be traffic today.
- The weather should be better this time of year.
- I should be skinnier this far into the diet.
- I should have gotten an A on the paper.

- She should give me a discount for the trouble.
- He should just quit bothering me all the time.
- I shouldn't be stuck at home.

These perceptions of what "should be" and what "shouldn't be" are not reality—they are merely the ways in which we see the world. They are falsehoods. They are not truths.

Holding onto and feeling frustrated about these beliefs, especially the ones that we cannot control—like traffic, train delays, weather, or global politics—causes so much unnecessary anguish. It also prevents us from moving forward. As long as we are trapped in our beliefs and disappointment, we cannot become Thrivers and get to where we want to go.

We must continually reevaluate our thoughts and release our mental delusions and expectations. When we are disappointed, we should ask ourselves:

- What am I becoming upset about?
- What wrong ideas am I holding on to?
- What are my expectations that I am not meeting?
- What am I spending time worrying about that I cannot control?
- What can I do about what I can control?

We must identify and question how and when we developed these illusions. Once identifying them, let them go. These falsehoods trick us into believing lies. They don't allow us to execute on what we can control in our lives.

There Will Always Be Great, Good, and Bad

Finally, we should know this: By the natural order of things, there will always be a percentage of things that go well, a percentage of things that go well enough, and a percentage of things that go terribly wrong. There will be milestones we accomplish and blow out of the water and others that we miss by a long shot. We tend to make our negative experiences and setbacks worse than they are and to fixate on them. We play them over and over again in our heads and give ourselves a mental beating. We should let it go! Let's move forward and continue towards thriving.

Feelings Do Not Determine True Progress

In general, as a principle, feelings are not a good way to measure how we're doing in life since they fluctuate day to day and even hour to hour. Instead, hard evidence, facts, and figures are the best way to measure progress. Feelings are all over the place and can switch at any given moment. We must change the way we measure our progress and shoot for consistent improvement over reasonable amounts of time. More on this in Book Two when we discuss the Second Pillar of Thriving: Effective Execution.

Outside Forces

Many of us tend to allow external forces to overly influence our feelings, which results in us giving them too much consideration when determining our actions. What is both scary and unfortunate is that making decisions based on our feelings is not always what is best for us, and the action is likely not representative of our best selves that seek to thrive.

- I feel unappreciated at work. → I should quit.
- I feel bored at school. → I should drop out.
- I don't feel committed to my relationship. → We should break up.
- I don't feel happy today. → There is something wrong with my life.
- My ex-boyfriend showed up at the dinner party. → I cannot stay. I have to leave.
- I just received bad news from work. → My day is ruined.
- She smirked after informing me it's going to rain on my honeymoon. → I can't stand her.
- My parents told me I'm not working hard enough. → I'm done trying.

The feelings that pop up in our lives from events and encounters like the ones above are very natural and prevalent in our everyday experience. To deal with the feelings that unexpectedly appear inside of us and prevent them from negatively influencing our decisions and behavior, we must properly deal with the random events that provoke us in our daily encounters.

Life is Irritating

Before discussing strategies to contend with life's difficult and annoying moments, we must first acknowledge the irritating thoughts, people, and events that ruin our blissful moments. We must embrace them and accept them because they will never go away. Unfortunately, these nuisances are part of life and are to be expected. We will never have those perfect, peaceful, dreamy lives we fantasize about. We should not be trying to avoid these moments. Annoyance and anxiety are almost inevitable at any point, and we should not assume there will ever be smoothness in our lives.

Sounds terrible and depressing? Well, it shouldn't. We can still have a great time. We can still achieve everything and anything we want. We can enjoy the pleasures in life. The beauty of accepting the inevitability of challenges in life is that we will never be blindsided by what life throws at us. We become capable of handling anything and everything without surprise or distress and move forward from every encounter without disrupting the joy we have in other areas of life. Nothing should ever be a threat to us enjoying our experience.

Owning Our Mood

If an obstacle pops up, say on your wedding day or at your dream job interview, you should take mental action to minimize the challenging force. Think, "What mindset do I want to be in?" or, "What do I want to be thinking about right now?" You could actualize what you want and how you want to be feeling at the moment. You are never stuck in the mood you're in. Unless, of course, you're relying on the outside world to determine your feelings.

Be under the influence of your own mood. Be comment-proof. Don't concentrate on not letting something or someone bother you. Instead, focus and concentrate on creating the experience you want to experience right now. Instead of consciously trying to ignore what is bothering you, enjoy everything else beyond what is there and irritating. You can enjoy in the face of aggravation. You can enjoy a movie while having a common cold. You can still enjoy a dinner date with a bruised shoulder injury.

In the same way, you can tackle your agenda for the day despite annoying obstacles.

Imagine yourself surrounded by an invisible protective shield. It is completely under your control and it does not allow external forces to make contact with you or your spirit. The shield is see-through and it allows you to properly experience and assess everything happening around you, but you decide what to let in and what to keep out. People, events, and even thoughts in your mind are entirely blocked from reaching you unless you choose to let them in. This shield can also defend against your unwanted feelings.

You own this protective shield and can use it wisely to your advantage. Remind yourself that you have this powerful shield, this strong line of defense and that you do indeed control what comes in or stays out. You decide what to let in and choose what affects your mood and feelings. Over time, the shield will be your greatest tool and will protect and preserve your experience of life and your inner spirit.

Scrambling Our Experience

A sure way to powerfully influence our feelings is to scramble our experience or to break our patterns. Breaking patterns automatically alters our moods because it refocuses our attention to other things that make us feel differently.

For example, let's say you are walking home from school feeling upset about your performance on an exam that day, and you're also stressing about having to study for tomorrow's exam. As you dwell on your terrible situation, a man runs up to a woman walking near you and steals her purse. She screams, and he runs off. Almost automatically, you suddenly chase after the man and rip the purse from his grip. The mugger runs off into the distance, and you walk back proudly to give the woman her purse. She yelps with joy, gives you a big hug, and thanks you for saving the day. Now, on your way home again, you feel different. You're not nearly the same person you were five minutes beforehand with the feelings of sadness and frustration. You may still be concerned about your grades and upcoming exams, but you're feeling good, you're projecting confidence. You will likely feel like a hero all day, if not all week. This is a scramble in your experience.

Since most of us will not have opportunities to be purse-saving superheroes, how could we realistically scramble our experiences and break our patterns? Well, have you ever been in an argument with someone and suddenly the doorbell rings? Have you ever felt anxious and suddenly your best friend calls you with great news or with fun plans to include you in? Almost every time these breaks happen, we never return to the state of mind we were in before the scramble.

Of course, you do not need to wait for external forces to present an opportunity to break your patterns; you can do this by yourself! Leave your house when you're feeling complacent. Go for a walk when you're feeling frustrated. Play music or watch a movie when you're feeling sad. Call a friend when you're feeling lonely. Write a gratitude journal when you're feeling anxious.[17] Go do something. Anything.

Just Do It!

There are times when we cannot do what we feel like doing and must instead do what we know needs to be done. Many of us

---

[17] Write down three things you're grateful for, or about three people you appreciate and love. You can even write down three things you're proud of about yourself!

wait for the perfect time to do something, postponing action until we feel just right about doing the task at hand. However, if we sit by uncompromisingly waiting until we feel a certain way to execute, nothing will get done and we will miss other opportunities in life. Many of the feelings we're waiting for usually come after the action is taken, or once the task is complete. We feel focused and engaged in school as we attend class. We feel happy and fulfilled in life only after we begin taking action on our goals. We feel motivated and confident to go to the gym *after* we start our workout routine. "Feeling" like we can't start or don't want to begin our activities are just deceptive tricks our minds use to keep us from taking action. We can do and want to do most things we know to be right. Sometimes we just need to do it.

TOOL #4:
TURNING PROBLEMS INTO PUZZLES

A man is sleeping in a chair. Suddenly, he wakes up alarmed, abruptly jumps from his chair, and runs to turn on a light switch. He hurries to look out the window, panics from what he sees, and then kills himself. What happened?[18,19]

This strange and mysterious tale is a very popular riddle that usually takes a group of five approximately 20-30 minutes to solve. The group is only allowed to ask yes or no questions, one question at a time, and slowly but surely, the group learns enough details surrounding the story to form a conclusive narrative that

---

[18] The rules of the riddle are as follows: Participants can only ask yes or no questions, such as, "Is it nighttime?" "Is he in his home"? "Did he see an airplane outside the window?" etc. Participants cannot ask any other types of questions. The one giving the riddle can only answer three ways: "yes," "no," or "irrelevant." The objective is for participants to ask smart questions whose answers would provide them more detail surrounding the story. It usually takes participants about 20-30 minutes to arrive at the solution, although the one giving the riddle could choose to set a time limit or leave it open-ended.

[19] *Riddle Solution:* The man sleeping in the chair was a lighthouse attendant on duty operating the lighthouse. His responsibility was to turn on the light at dark so that ships could navigate successfully, but, regrettably, he fell asleep on the job. When he woke up alarmed, realizing that he had fallen asleep, he quickly ran to turn on the lighthouse light and to look out the window. To his dismay, he saw a ship had crashed and that hundreds of people were drowning. He then killed himself.

allows them to solve the riddle. While dozens of different groups complete the riddle, ranging from classrooms to cocktail parties, the participant experience is always the same: they are focused, they are engaged, and they are entertained.

Think of the last time you had to solve a riddle. Were you focused and deliberate in your analysis, or were you guessing a bit more wildly? What about the last time you played a board game? Did you play Monopoly or Risk? Backgammon or chess? Think back to where you were and with whom you were playing. What were you feeling? How were your breathing and your heart rate? Were your eyes moving fast or were they locked in and focused? Were you sitting quietly in place still as stone, or were you jumping around yelling passionately? Whatever you were playing, and with whomever you were playing, it is very likely that you were super engaged and very entertained. Absorbing activities, from riddles and board games to sports and video games, are exciting and gripping. There is competition, there is intensity, and there are strategy and luck.

Think back to the last thrilling movie you saw. Revisit the most gripping story you've ever heard. Recall the times you worked to solve a word puzzle, a Rubik's cube, or a Sudoku problem. The mystery captures you; your curiosity is piqued, and you are tapped into a state of interest and flow that is hard to break. Why? Because your brain loves a good challenge, and even more so, your brain loves solving problems.

In life, we encounter many problems. We have setbacks at work, complications in our relationships, and troubles with health. At times, these burdens accumulate, becoming an overwhelming opponent that crushes us into helplessness. However, if we take a moment to look at our troubles for what they are, we realize that they are just problems that, like any other, need to be solved. The reason we are great at giving advice and solving other people's problems is that we love the stimulating challenge of solving a puzzle. Now, challenge yourself to view your problems as such, and then take them on with courage and vigor rather than with displeasure and frustration.

The next time an obstacle lands in your way, look at it with the mindset that it is just another interesting problem that you need to solve. It's a riddle, filled with engaging complexity and hidden opportunity. It's a game where your brain and body are stimulated and where the stakes are high. The thrill is real, and you're on a journey to solve the problem and complete the mission and then move forward onto the next level.

Solving the problem doesn't mean overanalyzing the issue and obsessively worrying to the point that you ignore other aspects of your life. It means thinking strategically, planning deliberately, and slowly implementing a course of action that brings you closer and closer to the solution.

Your biggest customer just dropped you as a provider? How can you work to win the customer back, bring on a better client, or increase business to hit the same revenue goals?

You just got a foot injury while training for a marathon? Okay, how can you modify your training to stay in shape or heal quickly so that you can compete as soon as possible?

Your professor dropped a last-minute assignment on you that's due the night before a big basketball game? Fine, are there ways you could juggle both responsibly and fit the assignment into your practice schedule so you could work on it as efficiently as possible?

Your boyfriend broke up with you right before prom? How can you move onwards productively in your life and find a new and interesting date who knows how to dance and keep up a conversation?

These are all familiar, relatable problems that pop up in each of our lives. We usually take them seriously, or panic, and many times we wish we never had to deal with them. Truth be told, we should be happy we have them. Scratch that—we should low-key love them. Why? Because they are good for us. They keep us thinking, they keep life interesting, and they force us to navigate life with a curious mind and the ability to problem-solve. Problems make us learn new things, try new things, and create new things. They force us to utilize our strengths, improve our weaknesses, and deploy our resources. Why do business people, professional athletes, and performers voluntarily take on more responsibility and stressful pressure? Why do leaders consciously leave their comfort zone? Well, because they love it! It's thrilling. They want more problems because they enjoy solving them. They enjoy the process of taking on more work for themselves because it puts them to the test and helps them reach the next level.

We should look at our problems the same way. They are fun (and serious), engaging (and exhausting), and exciting (and scary) challenges that we need to solve—and they help us grow! The only way to thrive is to have something to thrive in, on, or through. Problems provide us all of those! Problems allow us to put who we are and what we have to the test, and they help us achieve more. We learn what we're good at, what we could be better at, and how to thrive and make it to the next level.

While we think we don't want problems, the reality is that it couldn't be farther from the truth. People with no problems are bored. People with no problems are aimless. People with no problems are usually dead. If we want to be alive and growing as people, we need problems. We need newness and thrill. Without them, we sit in our comfort zones, staring blankly into the future, waiting to die. Why do anything if we have no reason or purpose?

With problems, we are sparked into action and forced to seek truth and clarity. There is no greater pleasure than overcoming a challenge or solving a problem. That is the purest thrill.

As life coach legend Steve Chandler points out in his book Reinventing Yourself, during wartime, suicides are at an all-time low. This is because a country's citizens are busy during wartime, contributing their energy towards a meaningful higher cause and purpose. People are motivated and have a passionate goal to attain. When we are on our deathbeds thinking back on our lives, we are not going to wish we had fewer problems and more comfort. We are going to wish we thrived more.[20]

The Problem with Problems

While the above seems like a gentle and effective way to look at our problems (it is, by the way; try it), the reason we are so fearful of problems is that they are typically brutal and erupt out of nowhere, completely capsizing us. We suddenly hear a loved one is diagnosed with a deadly disease. We find out that our significant other has been unfaithful for years. Our alcoholic, abusive parents lose their jobs and cannot afford the mortgage on our house anymore. Whatever our imaginations could come up with, real or fake, we know life has very disruptive and terrifying problems popping up all the time. How could we look at these as fun, exciting riddles?

Well, we don't. Certain problems are only excruciating. They pierce us and throw us into dark chaos. We question our beliefs, our abilities, and our lives. It hurts when we wake up, and it hurts when we go to sleep. We would rather avoid the problems and

---

[20] Chandler, Steve. Reinventing Yourself: How to Become the Person You've Always Wanted to Be. Career Press, 2017.

instead focus on what makes us happy because every time we even think about the problem we face, we suffer.

Face It

The only way to overpower the pain of a problem is to face it. To confront it and to take action towards fixing it. Ignoring and avoiding a problem makes it bigger and stronger and only more difficult to contend with. No matter how much we wish to move on in our lives and forget about the problem, the fact is the problem will not disappear. It will only stay and intensify. The problem will grow and find us. And when it does, it will be scarier and more painful. Therefore, we should contend with the problem while it is still developing and manageable. We should confront the problem while it is fresh. We are way stronger than we realize and must prove it to ourselves by staring what we fear in the face.

Take a Stand

Take a stand because running will only make us weaker, allowing problems to grow stronger. Fight the good fight, because if we win, we grow. If we lose, we grow. It's a win-win. It hurts, but we learn to cope. We would rather thrive than survive, and that means facing the problem despite the fear and pain we feel. Survivors live through hardship and disaster and feel damaged by trauma. Thrivers feel the same but show consequent growth and act with strength. Survivors and Thrivers experience the same event—the difference is how they bounce back, grow, and process the event.[21]

[21] Mangelsdorf, Judith, and Michael Eid. "What Makes a Thriver? Unifying the Concepts of Posttraumatic and Postecstatic Growth." *Frontiers*, Frontiers, 28 May 2015, www.frontiersin.org/articles/10.3389/fpsyg.2015.00813/full.

When we face a painful problem, we must not lose perspective. We cannot let it be our ultimate ruin, the destruction of our lives. We should deal with the specific problem head-on and face the chaos it brings to whatever particular area of our lives that it attacks. We must not let the particular problem we face affect the order in the rest of our lives. The chaos from our problem will try to penetrate other areas of our lives and force even the most stable foundations in our lives to crumble to dust. We must compartmentalize the problem and fight it. We must try to build order to combat the chaos. More importantly, we must keep the problem in its place and preserve our order in other areas of life.

If we need to take care of a loved one with an illness, we should do so with our best effort and with courage, despite the pain we feel along with it. When we're not actively dealing with the challenge or the task at hand, we should still be spending time with other people we love and continue doing the things we enjoy. If we discover our loved one has been unfaithful, we must not allow our whole life to come tumbling down. We must deal with the chaotic mess where it stands: in the relationship. We will continue to maintain the order we built in our other areas of life—our careers, our friendships, and our meaningful activities. All painful problems must be faced this way.

TOOL #5:
YOU'RE NOT STRESSED, YOU'RE EXCITED

We all experience stress. We stress about work, we stress about health, and we stress about performing in our lives. Although countless books, articles, talks, and calming techniques attempt to help us control our stress, we are more stressed than ever, running frantically in a busy world bombarded by social media pings, flashy advertising, and greater pressure to achieve "success."

While some of the creative methods proposed over the decades may lower feelings of stress moment to moment,[22] we know for sure that our stress is never going to disappear. Why? Because we're up against millions of years of evolution.[23]

When we're nervous before a big exam, anxious about an important interview, or worrying about an upcoming date, our minds are in survival mode. It is not because we're concerned that our teacher is going to eat us (that would be mean), but because we are subconsciously aware that there are consequences to our performance in life.

---

[22] Have you ever heard of a beer bath? Yep, it's been advised to bathe in beer to relieve stress. Google it!

[23] See Chapter on Intrusive Thoughts

A Stressful Misconception

While most people spend their entire lives believing that stress is bad, science is now proving that stress is very good sometimes, especially for our performance. When? When we stop trying to get rid of it and instead use stress to our advantage.

It is true; doctors and therapists claim that stress increases the risk for every illness under the sun. While the data does suggest that stress hurts our cardiovascular and immune systems, we are beginning to realize that it is not stress per se that is causing problems: it is the amount of stress, the way we look at the stress, and the way we manage it.[24]

Stress vs. Excitement

We have all felt our nerves ignite because of a stressful situation—like speaking publicly or taking our first big exam. Our hearts pound in our chests, our breathing speeds up, and sweat begins to form on our faces. We hope to ourselves that we're not losing our minds, and we tell ourselves that we're okay. But the anxiety keeps settling in. Our hands get clammy and cold, and we begin to panic. We realize we are anxious, and we try to stop the chaos happening in our heads. The pressure builds, and we tell ourselves to calm down and relax. We pray to God that no one notices how nervous we are. We try a breathing exercise. It doesn't work. We realize we cannot compose ourselves. Suddenly, we're freaking out. We're in a cycle of stress worrying to a fault about whether or not we will ruin our performance.

Now, what if we took this exact situation and flipped it on its head? What if instead, we decide to perceive our stress

---

[24] 24 McGonigal, Kelly. "How to Make Stress Your Friend." *TED*, www.ted.com/talks/ kelly_mcgonigal_how_to_make_stress_your_friend/up-next?language=en.

response—this fast-changing physiological response—as something that is actually good for our performance. What if we decide to use the stress as a means to make us more effective? Our pounding hearts prepare us for action and increase blood flow to our brains, enhancing our focus and cognitive abilities. Our faster breathing brings more oxygen to our lungs to feed our bodies' peak states. Our sweat is our body warming up as we zone in on the task at hand. This is the relationship with stress we want. We want to reframe the stress as excitement that boosts us. We're not stressed, we're excited. In this world, we become stronger, better, and faster in the face of our performance rather than panicked. We enter a flow state.

How We Think About Stress Matters

There is no doubt that stress is essential. Science has proven countless times that the right amount of stress is critical for peak performance. There is a law (it's called the Yerkes-Dodson Law and is named after the scientists who conducted the experiments) that shows too little stress is just as bad as too much stress. Both too much stress and too little stress hinder performance, learning, and creativity. The right amount of stress, however, has enormous benefits.

Why? Well, when we aren't stressed enough, we pay less attention and have less interest in the tasks at hand. Stress is needed as a stimulant to arouse motivation in us to perform and execute. Too much stress, on the other hand, can impair our performance due to overanxiety and nerves.[25]

---

[25] Gino, Francesca. "Are You Too Stressed to Be Productive? Or Not Stressed Enough?" *Harvard Business Review*, 5 Oct. 2017, hbr.org/2016/04/are-you-too-stressed-to-be -productive-or-not-stressed-enough.

If we adopt the belief that a stress response is helpful for performance, we will be less stressed out overall, less anxious, and more confident. Our heart rates and blood vessels will also remain at healthier levels. Chronic stress is usually related to cardiovascular disease because intensely stressful situations make people's heart rates go up, and their blood vessels constrict. Physiologically, this is not healthy when it occurs often. However, in a study where participants reframed stress as helpful, their physical profiles imitated joy and excitement, where their hearts still pounded, but their blood vessels did not constrict. Voila!

People who experience a lot of stress have varying results with their health depending on how they believe the stress affects them. People with high levels of stress who believe stress is harming them have a significantly higher risk of physiological issues. Alternatively, stressed people who view stress as harmless have the lowest risk of physiological injury, even less risk than those people who have little to no stress.[26] Think about that. That's mind-blowing.

Stress is Very Useful

The most important thing to note here is not only that we can handle the stress that comes with the challenges in life. The crucial lesson here is that stress helps us learn and grow and stay productive. Many times, we feel our stress disrupts our peace and comes from things beyond our control, against our will, or without purpose. This perception is what makes stress, well… stressful. Just remember, stress is only a natural signal that we're stepping outside of our comfort zones to solve an exciting puzzle

---

[26] McGonigal, Kelly. "How to Make Stress Your Friend." *TED*, www.ted.com/talks/ kelly_mcgonigal_how_to_make_stress_your_friend/up-next?language=en.

and to find valuable solutions to important questions. As odd as it may sound, stress does not have to be stressful, but we have to reframe it in a certain way. Stress will not kill us unless we believe it will. Stress will help us thrive in life and prime us for the task, but only if we let it.

The next time we feel stressed, we should remind ourselves that this physiological and psychological response is positive and is readying our minds and bodies to perform at peak levels. Once we become accustomed to this relationship with stress, this far healthier perspective will come naturally and we will never be worried about stress again.

TOOL #6:
DON'T GET CRAZY ABOUT CRITICISM

On May 10, 1996, 23 people climbed Mount Everest's summit under the leadership of climbing legends Rob Hall and Scott Fischer. It was a challenging climb—teammates deteriorated in health, guides did not follow protocol, and leaders improperly prepared for the weather and the needed supplemental oxygen. A few days earlier, however, Hall had made it clear that no one was to question his judgment: "I will tolerate no dissension up there. My word will be absolute law, beyond appeal. If you don't like a particular decision I make, I'd be happy to discuss it with you afterward, but not while we're up on the hill.[27]"

As a result, expedition members were afraid to speak up to the leaders and to question their decisions. They were indoctrinated not to correct mistakes, challenge superiors, or present criticism. When climbers noticed Fischer's deteriorating health during the ascent, no one questioned his plans to proceed. Neal Beidleman, an expedition guide gravely concerned that the climb would pass their set turnaround time, did not feel comfortable telling Fischer they should turn around.

---

[27] Jon Krakauer, *Into Thin Air* (New York: Anchor Books, 1998), pp. 216–217

Fischer did not sincerely acknowledge any concerns, including the lack of experience of his expedition members. Fischer replied to a journalist, "Experience is overrated. We've got the big E figured out."[28] He also said: "I believe 100 percent that I'm coming back. . . My wife believes 100 percent that I'm coming back. She isn't concerned about me at all when I'm guiding because I'm [going to] make all the right choices.[29]"

Tragically, by the end of the day, both Hall and Fischer had died on the descent along with three other expedition members. They were caught in a violent storm and were unable to return to base camp before dark. Sadly, those who survived felt a pang of mutual guilt that they should have spoken up and could have potentially prevented the disaster. The biggest hazard on the mountain turned out to be that there was no communication, no questioning of assumptions, and no criticism.

Criticism is Critical

For most of us, criticism is a tough pill to swallow. Although parts of us know that the feedback found in criticism is helpful to us, we tend not to process or respond constructively to criticism. We take comments about our behavior or performance personally and feel as though our character or identity is being attacked.

There are, in fact, times where we are being attacked, as many people do not understand the right way to provide useful feedback. Nonetheless, it is established that the input found in the right type of criticism is crucial to learning, improvement, and development.

---

[28] Krakauer, pp. 85–86
[29] Krakauer, p. 84

We each have to contend with our inner ego. Legendary investor and philanthropist Ray Dalio describes our egos and blindspot barriers as our biggest obstacles to thriving. He says our egos prevent us from acknowledging our weaknesses honestly, and our need to be right overpowers our need to be true. This is dangerous and unfortunate since we are beings with great power to become better, but thoughtlessly choose not to. He reminds us that we all have blind spots, and none of us can see everything, both about the world and about ourselves. No one alone can see a full picture of reality; therefore, we need others and their criticism to push us to thrive and make better decisions in life.[30]

Unfortunately, we tend to draw ourselves towards friends and family that act as our "cheerleaders" and support us no matter what. While outside validation is comforting and useful, it is just as important to have honest friends and family who call us out when we're wrong and tell us the truth without sugarcoating it. Instead of avoiding sincere people who challenge us and criticize us, we should invite in individuals who will say to us the things we do not want to hear but need to hear. Wharton organizational psychologist Adam Grant calls it a "Challenge Network" and explains that to benefit from one, we must be willing to listen. To be the best, we must be prepared to face criticism and learn from feedback, right or wrong. To be a Thriver, our results and progress must be more important than our self-images at the moment.[31]

Looking at the scenario involving the Everest climb, it is clear that ego and overconfidence are powerful forces to reckon with

---

[30] "Principles for Success." Performance by Ray Dalio, *Principles by Ray Dalio*, www. principles.com/principles-for-success/#.

[31] TED. "How to Love Criticism." *Work Life with Adam Grant*, Season 1, Episode 1, Apple Podcasts App, 28 Feb. 2018.

and potentially dangerous if not held in check. They are blinding, and denying criticism in a world of complexity leaves us vulnerable to unexpected forces or problems that others with different perspectives would provide us if welcomed. By greeting opposing ideas and exploring alternatives, we can both test and validate our viewpoints and ensure we are doing the best we can.

Bad Criticism

There is indeed "bad" criticism. Bad criticism attacks the individual personally. It is not specific and does not provide any real actionable feedback that the person could use to improve.[32]

Attacks on the Individual

From time to time, we all hear comments that accuse us of having undesired personality traits. For example:

- "You're so antisocial."
- "You're very selfish."
- "You're so unprofessional."

There are times we brush these comments off like nothing, and there are other times we feel enraged or hurt by the criticism. We feel personally attacked, and our defense mechanisms immediately go up. This is because the person is criticizing our identities rather than specific conduct. These comments imply that we are "antisocial," "selfish," or "unprofessional" by our very nature, intrinsically as people, at all times, and in all areas of life. Rather

---

[32] Cannon, Mark D., and Robert Witherspoon. "Actionable Feedback: Unlocking the Power of Learning and Performance Improvement." *Academy of Management Perspectives*, vol. 19, no. 2, 2005, pp. 120–134., doi:10.5465/ame.2005.16965107.

than understanding precisely what we did and where we could improve, we feel that our character is attacked, our personalities are flawed, and in turn, we respond emotionally and unproductively. There is no motivation to change for the better, and we either ignore the feedback or attack back.

Criticism Lacking Specificity or Examples

Are we always antisocial? Or are we antisocial only when our group of friends asks to go partying? Are we selfish to everyone? Or have we been selfish to our significant others lately? Are we unprofessional in all areas of life and at all times? Or have we just been dressing unprofessionally over the summer because it's been sweltering outside, and we prefer not to wear a three-piece suit to sales meetings? Non-specific criticisms like "you're so antisocial," "you're very selfish," or "you're so unprofessional" do not provide nuanced feedback to us for correct interpretation. Consequently, we become defensive and exclaim that the comments are all false accusations. "We went for dinner with your friends three times last month!" "I bought you flowers for your birthday!" and "I am so professional! I always send calendar invites and confirmation emails to our clients!" These are potential defenses to the overarching critiques above and show that criticism that does not accurately state the problem at hand is bound to be received with anger and claims that the criticism is false and unwarranted.

Criticism Lacking Meaning

Why is this criticism significant? What are the consequences of the wrong behavior? What is the purpose of the feedback? Why is it meaningful? What are the next steps or ways to fix the problem? Comments like "you're so antisocial," "you're very selfish," or "you're so unprofessional" do not provide any worthwhile criticism in terms of why the behavior is problematic. Are we missing out on fun goings-on by being antisocial? What are the exciting activities we could do to enjoy spending more time with people? Are we hurting people by being selfish? How could we be more considerate to the people we may have offended? Are we losing out on revenue and potential customers because of our unprofessional demeanor or clothing? Is there any way we could be more professional in how we dress while at the same not being stifled by the sweltering heat? These details must be included in the criticism so the receivers logically recognize the areas of improvement and can put steps in place to progress and take corrective action.

Good Criticism

Good criticism confronts a person's undesirable behaviors and correctly points out when the behaviors occurred. Furthermore, good criticism mentions why the behaviors were harmful and ways in which the person could improve.[33]

Giving Feedback

If we want to tell someone something like, "you're so antisocial," "you're very selfish," or "you're so unprofessional," we should look for ways to refine and better deliver the criticism. Instead of attacking a person with a statement like, "You're so antisocial," offer a solution and plan of action. For example, "I feel we would enjoy spending more time with our friends. Let's have them for dinner, and I'll make your favorite lasagna you've been

[33] Cannon, Mark D., and Robert Witherspoon. "Actionable Feedback: Unlocking the Power of Learning and Performance Improvement." *Academy of Management Perspectives*, vol. 19, no. 2, 2005, pp. 120–134., doi:10.5465/ame.2005.16965107.

asking for." Instead of saying, "You're very selfish," site a specific example of selfish behavior. For example, "It was hurtful when you, my husband, chose to spend my birthday with your friends instead of with me. It was wrong. I am upset, and I was so lonely. You should have at least reserved part of the day for me." Instead of saying, "You're so unprofessional," take the lead in inspiring change. For example: "I believe we would perform better in the sales meetings if we both dressed more professionally. Let's wear nicer shoes and short-sleeve button-downs instead of t-shirts."

These kinds of feedback do not attack nor put the blame directly on the person but instead, specify the problems and offer productive and constructive suggestions. This is the form of criticism we should work to provide.

Receiving Feedback

If and when someone gives us bad criticism, we must remind ourselves of this common criticism-giving trap and neither take it personally nor attack the feedback giver. We should respond in turn with clarifying questions to fully understand and identify where the problem lies, and how—if necessary—we could improve. This includes taking a step back and assessing both ourselves and the possible meaning that could be hiding in the criticism. "Can you please point out the times when you feel I am antisocial?" "Can you please explain to me why you think I am selfish?" "When, specifically, have I been unprofessional?" These questions allow the feedback giver to polish their criticism and boil it down into informative pieces of intelligence that we could use to better ourselves.

Personal Learning Versus Interpersonal Learning

Feedback complements personal learning and presents an opportunity for us to learn more about ourselves and the world around us through others. While personal learning focuses on reflection and introspection, interpersonal learning focuses on learning with and from others. After all, we need others to know ourselves.

It is important that we develop healthy relationships with feedback, otherwise, we risk losing its benefits and purpose. We must take our defensive armor off, as others may come to disguise their sincere reactions towards us out of fear of upsetting, hurting, or offending us. People tend to avoid conflict. We should aspire to have people engage truthfully with us so that we may continue to grow. On the other hand, we also mustn't obsess over the feedback we receive.

There are moments where people we respect, admire, or fear provide us with strong feedback that we hold onto even way after we have reconciled the subject at hand. Many times, this feedback comes from parents or siblings, and it hurts us for years. We must learn to acknowledge when we have improved in areas we were once critiqued and move onwards. There is no value in holding onto obsolete feedback that no longer applies.

We must understand that accepting feedback does not mean we are inferior beings. Acknowledging feedback does not mean we admit to being incompetent or unrespectable. Feedback is simply another data point we use to assess and decide our next steps. Hearing a person's suggestion or criticism does not imply or require that we make the change or agree with the assessment.

Similarly, providing criticism to important people in our lives is neither offensive nor mean-spirited. Feedback, when given properly and effectively, is quite the contrary. It is a sign of confidence in that person's ability to change and it should be appreciated by the receiver. We need not fear to compromise our relationships or to hurt others if we give the feedback clearly, compassionately, and sincerely.

TOOL #7:
TRICKS TO BUILD CONFIDENCE

The air is quiet and still on a July afternoon in the lush grasslands of Kenya. The wind is light and the sun is shining gold-orange in the clear African sky. The wildebeest migration is at its peak, and hungry predators lurk in the brush.

BBC and its film crew have been surveying the area—they are looking to capture an incredible yet dangerous tradition of the local Maasai people: stealing food from lions. Practiced in Kenya for thousands of years, taking the kill of other creatures proved an efficient way for humans to acquire local catch. After all, competing with fast and strong Kenyan predators is no easy undertaking.

Today, three Maasai locals have identified their target—a freshly killed wildebeest ready for the taking. The catch: 15 hungry lions surround the animal, munching away on its remains. The leader of the group is Rakita. He is 65 years old and has a lot of experience both hunting and warding off lion attacks. He analyzes the lions carefully, very well aware that the task at hand is life-threatening. They must approach the apex predators with the utmost confidence. Intimidating a pack of lions is a challenging task given that lions do not fear other predators and attack the biggest of creatures—elephants, giraffes, and wildebeests.

As Rakita observes his opponents, his body is tense. His heart pounds deeply in his chest, and a chilling sweat glides down his face. He feels the earth between his toes and the breeze along his rigid face. The lions munch away, noses covered in blood.

Rakita knows that the time to confront the lions is now and that they must do so with strength and unity. They swiftly stand up tall from the grass and immediately start walking towards the lions in unison. The lions look up and growl, but Rakita and his buddies are undeterred and continue their brisk pace towards the lions. They hold their breath and their hearts still pound away while their eyes remain fixed on the lions. As they move in closer, the dominant male suddenly jumps up and runs into the trees, the other lions following close. Rakita moves fast and with focus, as he must complete the task before the lions recognize the bluff and retaliate against the raiders. They quickly cut meat from the prey and, within seconds, are off with their evening dinner. They have safely accomplished their mission—all while the hoodwinked and hungry lions witnessed the heist from only a few hundred yards away.[34]

Confidence = Brave Action in the Face of Risk

Confidence is the ability to take brave action in the face of challenges and prodding fear. Confidence is continuing to accomplish a goal despite the uncomfortable discouragement, slim odds, and painful adversity one confronts. While we all have confidence in certain areas, we could always use more. Becoming Thrivers and shooting for the stars involves dealing with struggles that increase in difficulty as we progress in life. Fortunately, there is a lot of

---

[34] ABC TV & iView. *Human Planet | Grasslands: Stealing Meat from the Mouths of Lions. YouTube*, YouTube, 18 Sept. 2017, www.youtube.com/watch?v=y3MTDFNf71I.

science (and many role models) to help us learn to become more confident.

Every Master Was Once a Fool

When we aspire to become Thrivers and achieve new goals, we and our confidence will inevitably face tests. We will never be fully confident nor fully content. This is the very nature of moving onwards and upwards when thriving. We take on more roles and responsibilities, we attempt to master new crafts, and we encounter novel ideas

Unsurprising to us, anything we face that is new or different requires a learning curve. We are doing something our brains have never done before. That is why we do terribly when we begin learning a new skill. However, we have to fail and fall if we are to advance. Yes, we will look like fools, but that's just how it works. Picasso could not have painted the art we admire today before he made years of terrible unnoticed work. Kobe Bryant could not have become one of the greatest ballplayers of all time before learning to dribble with his left hand. These greats recognized the inevitable learning curve and took the embarrassment that came with it. They remained focused and forward-thinking on their goals. While the people we look up to seem super-human, they are not. They are far from perfect. They exemplify specific virtues that we could learn from to become Thrivers just like them.

We're Not Any Different Than the People We Admire

People doing amazing things are no different from us. They just put tools and strategies to use. For those of us who learn violin for the first time, we will make terrible screeching sounds that will make us and anyone listening wince. Unless we're Gordon Ramsey, we will try cooking for the first time and make ourselves gag. This is just how it works. We must accept the struggle found at the beginning of any new venture. It is always hard to accept the possibility that we will mess up at a new job or in a new relationship. If we do, however, and we continue forward, there will be a turning point, and we will conquer the task at hand.

Preparation

The best way to develop confidence in any activity is by doing the activity over and over again. When we repeat a process, the deliberate practice forms our expertise over time, and we eventually begin to excel.

"The confidence comes from preparation. When the game is on the line, I'm not asking myself to do something that I haven't done thousands of times before. When I'm prepared, I know what I'm capable of doing, I know what I'm comfortable doing, and I know what I'm not comfortable doing. So, in those moments, if it looks like I'm ice cold or not nervous, it's because I've done it thousands of times before. So, what's one more time?"

– Kobe Bryant, NBA Basketball Champion.[35]

We have all had periods in our lives where we worked tirelessly to learn something new, like mastering a complicated technique, understanding a difficult concept, or performing a big task. It often seems impossible when we start practicing, but eventually, everything begins to click and we realize that we can nail it. As human beings, we aspire to conquer new undertakings all the time, whether it's reaching a high vocal note or learning the piano, surfing a big wave or hitting a home run, publishing a piece of writing or successfully delivering a famous speech. We practice for hours,

---

[35] Piotrekzprod. *The Mind of Kobe Bryant - Confidence. YouTube*, YouTube, 9 Oct. 2018, www.youtube.com/watch?v=iXciUuVQvTc.

days, months, and years, refining our methods, bettering our technique, until our performance feels entirely right. Whether we do so out of passion or because "practice makes perfect," it's from this deliberate practice that we become masters over what we do, and a whole lot of confidence comes along with it.

"Repetition is the father of learning. Intelligence...all that comes from repetition. Awareness, preparation...all that comes from repetition."

– Lil Wayne, Grammy-winning Rapper.[36]

Whenever we do anything, the cells in our brains (called neurons) fire electrical signals and form a neural network that helps us learn and perform the task faster. When we repeat the action over and over again, our brains reinforce the electrical pathways and the network becomes more efficient, making us way better at what we're doing.[37]

Unfortunately, one can't master a complicated task simply by repeating it over and over again for a few minutes or hours. The repetition needs to be spaced over a longer period of time with breaks in between. Neuroscientists have discovered that this "spaced repetition" is the best way to master a task.[38] For example, if a singer is looking to memorize a song for a big performance in two weeks, she should spread out her practice accordingly. She should practice the song a few times in the

[36] Exposure, Elevated. *Repetition Is the Father of Learning - Wise Words from Wayne. YouTube,* YouTube, 19 Mar. 2016, www.youtube.com/watch?v=uTINOGFv-Dw.

[37] Zatorre, Robert J et al. "Plasticity in gray and white: neuroimaging changes in brain structure during learning." *Nature neuroscience* vol. 15,4 528-36. 18 Mar. 2012, doi:10.1038/nn.3045.

[38] Kang, Sean H. K. "Spaced Repetition Promotes Efficient and Effective Learning: Policy Implications for Instruction." Policy Insights from the Behavioral and Brain Sciences, vol. 3, no. 1, Mar. 2016, pp. 12–19, doi:10.1177/2372732215624708.

morning and a few more times in the afternoon. She could then repeat the song before dinner and once more before bed. If she continues to practice the song like this—in intervals throughout the day—her brain will most effectively build its neural networks around the task.

"My confidence comes from my performance, my work in the gym, my work ethic…"

– Connor McGregor, UFC Champion[39]

Similarly, doing any activity over and over again makes you prepared and confident that you can excel at what you set out to do. If you have a big speech to deliver, practice it ten times in front of the mirror. Then practice on your friends and family. Practice it in a noisy room and a quiet room. Practice it when you're tired and when you're energetic. If you practice your task in this way, in a diverse set of situations and conditions, when the actual task presents itself, you will feel confident and ready to execute. You've seen it all. You've done it all.

Paint A Masterpiece

A masterpiece painting is the sum of a thousand brush strokes coming together into an awe-inspiring experience. We are no different. The great accomplishments we witness and those we dream for ourselves are an accumulation of countless moments of effort formed over the span of time.

Two Sides to The Confidence Coin

When it comes to confidence, there are two sides to the coin. On one side, there is having confidence in what we can control.

---

[39] Command, Charisma on. *How To Be More Confident - Connor McGregor Confidence Breakdown. YouTube*, YouTube, 30 Nov. 2015, www.youtube.com/watch?v=2CfFvtSUDA0.

This means preparation, hours of practice, and repetition of an activity to develop a comfort level for it. Our training is entirely in our control. If we have a speech, we practice the speech a lot. If we have a big basketball game, we practice our free-throws. If we're in a surf competition, we practice balance and flexibility. This preparation is essential to gain confidence when performing.

Uncertainty

On the other side of the coin, there is having confidence in the face of uncertainty—confidence when confronting what we can't control, like when we have a speech to give in class on Wednesday, but our professor suddenly decides we must do it Monday. As another example, we may have a big basketball game, but our contact lenses fall out during warmup, which means playing with eyeglasses. Similarly, imagine entering a surf competition only to find that the waves are bigger than we expected and there are more contestants than we had anticipated. These situations that pop up outside of our control exist in the realm of uncertainty, and we must learn to confront them confidently if we are to thrive.

Old News

The first step towards confidence in the face of uncertainty is recognizing that we have successfully handled similar situations in the past. Things popping up out of control that work to throw us off are merely life's old news. We've had to make last-minute decisions many times and have had to find last-minute solutions on the fly for things that randomly sprung up.

There were days where we missed our train to work and successfully improvised a way to get in on time or at least late, but undetected. There were times we were working on important projects and our computers crashed, but we magnificently found a way to submit the work on time—or receive an extension. There were moments we were expected to know answers to questions we didn't prepare for and either tactfully dodged the situation entirely or presented ideas we hadn't fleshed out yet. There were occasions where those we desired rejected us, those we respected criticized us, and those we cared about demoralized us, yet we continued on with our ambitions. We have overcome sicknesses, both mild and severe, and obstacles that have challenged us mentally and physically. We have dealt with endless setbacks in our academic careers, but we were able to get ourselves caught up in areas we were weak and behind. We have dealt with issues at work and wrestled with ambivalence regarding our jobs. We have lost loved ones—whether to death or to drifting away—and carried on. All in all, we have been through a lot, mostly what we could not expect, yet we made it out, broken in places, thriving in others.

We have all had periods in our lives where we felt cornered and confused and thought we would never persevere through the situation at hand, but did. We have each been in tough, complicated positions, where resolutions and relief seemed far away, but we pulled through and made it out okay anyway. We have all, at least once, mastered a skill, or made it through something that we thought, at the time, would be impossible. We just don't think about those times or give ourselves enough credit.

We must give ourselves that vital recognition. We deserve to. We love to brag about self-awareness and our strict judgment towards ourselves. We virtuously punish ourselves to become better people and look to self-correct. Well, the truest judges acknowledge the *truth*. So, we must also accept all that we have overcome. We must recognize our strengths and our successes, our comebacks and our progress.

While it is impossible to prepare for everything that could occur, it is possible to feel prepared for anything that does. Realizing that we have triumphed through uncertainty once before, should empower us and let us know we can do it again. We step away from the fear of the unknown and instead confront whatever the unknown has in store for us. Although there is no predicting nor preparing for the many different ways life could go wrong, we can trust that we will figure out how to handle the situation no matter what happens. We have all effectively dealt with unpredictable encounters in the past. Even in the instances when we did not, at least we survived and grew into better people for it.

Riding the Wave

Enthusiastic surfers have mastered keeping confidence in the face of uncertainty. While a surfer could practice swimming, improving balance, and developing flexibility, the reality is the surfer could never be truly prepared for everything the ocean has in store for them. The sea is a volatile, unpredictable force, and no two waves are ever the same. Surf break conditions, swells, weather, and other life in the water all influence the way a surfer experiences the ocean, and each time we venture out presents an opportunity for surprise.

Is it a beach break, point break, or reef break? Are there sharks, rays, or urchins? Is there a wind swell or a groundswell? How strong is the wind, and what direction is it blowing? Is the tide high or low? Are there strong currents and rips? Are the waves big or small? Are they sloping or steep? Fast or slow? Frequent or infrequent? Are the waves breaking left, right, or are they closing out? How many other surfers are there? Long boarders or short boarders? Is the surfboard glass or foam? Is it a long paddle out or a short one? Is there a channel to paddle out into? Are we wearing wetsuits or are we surfing bareback?

These are examples of the many questions a surfer must ask herself before a session at a new surf spot. It is evident that there are many elements outside of the surfer's control. How does the surfer still have confidence in the face of this uncertainty?

Let's take a young girl named Kayla, who is surfing the Soup Bowl surf spot in Barbados for the first time. On the east coast of Barbados in the town of Bathsheba, Soup Bowl is well-known among surfers because it produces some of the greatest reef-break waves in the world.

"I've been going for over 20 years, and I'd put Soup Bowl as one of the top three waves in the world," said Kelly Slater, 11-time surfing world champion. "The only problem is that there are sea urchins all over the bottom—just don't fall and you're fine."[40]

Along with its powerful and fast waves, Soup Bowls is notorious for its slicing reef covered in sharp sea urchins. When Soup Bowl's swell is big, surfers do not remotely think about sharks. They are too focused on not cracking their heads open and drowning in the massive surf.

In anticipation of her trip to Soup Bowl, Kayla has been preparing all winter, surfing her local spots on the East Coast and using tools and techniques daily to practice her balance, her breathing, and her flexibility. She plans to surf the swell big and intends to feel ready physically and mentally when she arrives in Barbados. She researches Soup Bowls before her trip and prepares for the sessions accordingly. She determines the best times to paddle out and brings the ideal boards and wetsuits for the

---

[40] Pergament, Danielle. "Surf's Up in Barbados." *The New York Times*, The New York Times, 27 Mar. 2009, www.nytimes.com/2009/03/29/travel/29barbados.html.

conditions. Sometimes she will bring multiple boards and leashes to each session, extra wax, and a first aid kit. Once she arrives at the surf spot, she watches the water. She determines the best place to paddle out, where she should sit to catch waves and the overall dynamic of the water. She even asks other surfers and locals about the spot. What should she look out for? How are the conditions there generally? She then does a quick stretch, puts her leash on, and jumps in.

Notice that Kayla made sure to do everything she could to be prepared for her sessions. While it is intimidating to surf a new spot with so much ambiguity, any avid surfer like Kayla will tell you that there is a thrill in the unknown. The mix of preparation, challenge, risk, and focus is what makes surfing so exciting. Kayla focuses on catching the right wave, but she also looks out for other surfers taking off before she does and other surfers paddling out. She glides down a fast wave in joy, but must also pay close attention to the rocky areas and ensure she exits the wave on time. Kayla admires the mesmerizing colors of the ocean and reef's surface but also stays aware of urchins, sharks, and other sea life.

How does Kayla mentally train to deal with these potential problems, the uncertainty, and the unknown? How does she keep her confidence? Well, this isn't Kayla's first time surfing a new surf spot. In the past, when she has surfed a new place for the first time, she nailed it. She had prepared well and successfully triumphed over the waves with no problem. In fact, she has done this most of the time on the water.

There have also been times, however, where Kayla only mastered a new spot after contending with scary obstacles and pressing issues that popped up along the way. She has wiped out badly before. She has collided with other surfers before. She has snapped her board in half. She has lost a leash. She has cut herself on the reef. She has encountered sharks. Unfortunately, she has even had one or two life-or-death moments, where the waves have held her down for almost too long and where she lost her board in big swell. The critical thing to recognize, however, is that she made it through those moments. She remained clearheaded and focused, and despite fear and a pounding heart, she did what she had to do to get herself out of those situations. Because Kayla is aware of her experience of having dealt with unpredictable obstacles in the past successfully (gracefully or not), she has the confidence to continue forward and to paddle on.

Surfs Up

As human beings, we are just like surfers. We must prepare as much as we can, but then embrace that life is uncertain and learn to love it. We must trust that our future selves can handle whatever the future throws at us since we have handled uncertainty in the past. Whether or not we made it through happily or healthily at the time, we made it through. No matter what happens or what situation we are put in, we must believe in our future selves to figure it out. Having this trust enables us to live and thrive even when confronted with uncertainty.

We're more likely to screw up our health, relationships, or business if we worry about screwing up. When Kayla is in the water, she isn't constantly thinking, "What if I crash into another surfer? What if I wipe out? What if a shark comes?" She focuses on surfing safely and intelligently. When she is riding a wave, she isn't paranoid about wiping out and hitting the reef. She focuses on riding the wave. When she is paddling out, she doesn't panic when the ocean throws her around. She doesn't look to fight the waves and resist the movement. She flows. She focuses on safely getting to where she needs to get. She stays clear and calm despite a pounding heart. If she panics in the face of waves and tries to resist them the waves will win. They will crash and crush her. Similarly, we must think about health to have health. We need to think love to have love. If we concern ourselves with losing health or losing love, we will ruin our present experience of health and love. As human beings, we tend to think we're helping ourselves by being extra cautious, but we're harming ourselves. Being extra cautious is going to get us into accidents. Imagine driving with a person who is paranoid about crashing! We would get out of that car as fast as possible. Where we focus is where we go. The uncontrollable nerves are what get us into trouble. This does not mean we cannot feel fear. We can! But we shouldn't focus on fear. We should focus on the task at hand. Execute.

- What if I get injured before the big game?
- What if I lose my voice before the concert?
- What if I can't sleep the night before my important interview and I can't perform?
- What if the crowd is bored and tired from all the other speakers and they tune out for my speech?
- What if my boss is too upset about this quarter's earnings when I ask for my raise next week?
- What if my date doesn't like me and never goes out with me again?

These are not the kinds of questions that we should be asking ourselves. Be aware that these things can happen and prepare accordingly but focus on executing the task at hand. Focus on achieving exactly your desired outcome as if nothing else is in your way. Practice hard for the big game, but intelligently. Repeat your singing act over and over, but also drink tea with honey and rest your voice intermittently. Prepare for your big interview and understand you will perform regardless of how much sleep you had. Practice your speech, and regardless of the crowd's energy, give it your all. Find the best time to approach your boss for your raise, get your talking points in order, and then give it your all. Enjoy your date, be yourself, and whatever happens next, so be it.

Trusting in our future selves also allows us to focus presently on what's in front of us. How could we effectively deal with our current problems today while we also carry the burdens of our future (or even our past)? We are likely to mess up working through the issues of today if we are also concerned with irrelevant potential anxieties of the future. "How will I get married if I can't even get a date?" "I better be a good parent because my parents were not there for me!" "How will I make enough money to support a family?" These are all concerns with the uncertainty that is not pressing for today. Tell yourself, "I believe and trust in my future self to figure it out. My future self will handle whatever happens. As long as I'm doing everything I can now, my future self will solve my future problems. I will presently handle my present self!"

If your mind tries to change your focus and fixate on thoughts about the things you already acknowledged and adequately prepared for, treat them as intrusive thoughts and apply the intrusive thought method. You must decide to not be coerced by the thoughts eroding at your confidence. Most people believe fearlessness is the absence of fear. Fearlessness, however, is not a quality or a state of being. It is an approach, one that you can use once you know the way. Make a decision. Nothing is going to spoil this moment. Detach yourself from whatever fear you're feeling.

Two of the Six Human Needs

After decades of experience and analysis, renowned life coach Tony Robbins determined there are six basic human needs—two of which are certainty and uncertainty.[41] Certainty provides us confidence and the comfort that our lives will be okay. This security, this safety, is critical. We generally want to be certain about our health, our safety, our money, and our relationships. Because life is ever-changing, to maintain our confidence and certainty, we must always be willing to prepare more, motivate ourselves, and change our expectations. If we do not, we may lose our confidence and become avoidant of new people and situations altogether. Therefore, let us prepare ourselves and accomplish the life we dream.

Uncertainty is critical because, without it, life can get boring. Without change, we become bored, complacent, and apathetic. The need for uncertainty is why we vary the people we hang out with, the hobbies we engage in, the food we eat, and the music we listen to. A midlife crisis is usually caused by having no variety. Variety is a need, not a want. If we were served the same food every day, we would probably get sick. Our minds and bodies alike need variety. Would we want to be the same people for the rest of our lives? We must find variety in our lives. We must find variety in our businesses, in our relationships, and in our interests or we become bored. Therefore, let us embrace the uncertainty in life and discover what it has in store for us.

Visualize

Thanks to neuroscience and its dedicated professionals, we have discovered an almost magical way that we can prepare for the

---

[41] Robbins, Tony. "6 Human Needs." *Tonyrobbins.com*, 25 July 2019, www.tonyrobbins.com/mind-meaning/do-you-need-to-feel-significant/.

unknown and build our confidence: visualization. It turns out, our brains and nervous systems do not differentiate between real memories and ones that are imagined like ones we visualize or dream.[42] This is why nightmares and horror movies can mess with us.

Furthermore, this truth reveals the power our imaginations can exert on our confidence and preparation. When we concentrate on vividly imagining and feeling an experience, our brains evolve and mold themselves accordingly, as though we experienced it in real life. This means that we can use our imaginations to "experience" many different situations that could occur, and then use those same visualizations to overcome and triumph. Doing this technique enough tricks our brains into making the unknown known. Our brains believe we went through the situation, learned from it, and stored the memory in preparation to take on similar challenges.

Fighting legend Connor McGregor applies this technique when preparing for a big fight. He visualizes every situation possible in the ring—from getting pinned to the floor, struggling while grappling with his opponent, and getting injured early on. He then visualizes how he would overcome each situation. He visualizes the techniques he deploys in each situation, the moves and methods he uses to tire and hurt his opponent, and his fighting stance and breathing throughout. By repeating these visualization techniques over and over again, McGregor prepares himself for every fight—any fight—before the match even happens. No matter what his opponent does or what happens in the ring, McGregor has thought of it and trained his brain to prepare for it as though he already went through the

---

[42] Schacter, Daniel L et al. "The future of memory: remembering, imagining, and the brain." *Neuron* vol. 76,4 (2012): 677-94. doi:10.1016/j.neuron.2012.11.001

experience. Lucky for us, we can implement the same visualiza-
tion technique for ourselves. If you are weeks away from giving a big speech, close your
eyes, and then visualize the experience. How many people are in
the audience? 50? 100? 500? Visualize as vividly as possible the
crowd and their expressions. See what they are wearing, how they
are behaving. What are you wearing? How are you feeling? How
is your posture? Your breathing? Do you feel air conditioning on
your face? Look around the room. Take in the details: the lights,
the walls, the chairs, the stage. Envision the whole layout. Feel
the floor underneath your feet and the papers in your hand. Hear
the MC introduce your name. Hear the applause from the crowd.
Touch the mic, feel the energy of the room, look at the crowd.
Now deliver the speech.

Incredibly, after you do this visualization a few times, you will
start to feel comfortable about giving the speech. Now, you could
spice things up a bit and visualize unpredictable hurdles coming your
way and handle them accordingly. There is a heckler in the crowd.
You're asked to speak last. Or first. You stain your tie. You lose your
voice or your papers. You blank. Whatever obstacles you fear or challenges you dread, visualize them in vivid detail. Don't just jump to
visualizing your desired outcome of saving the day—grapple with
the discomfort, the pain, the anxiety. Let those feelings begin to ter-
rify you, and then begin to work through the situation. How are you
going to handle it? Are you going to improvise? Pivot? Give it a go
and see what happens. Then see what you learned from it! And start
over. Use this time when you're visualizing to make mistakes, so you
learn and gain the relevant experience that prepares you for the real
thing. Use all five of your senses in your visualization.

The goal is not to get carried away in visualizing things going
wrong. The goal is for you to get it right. Visualize the situation

and how you imagine it looks like when you're achieving what you want (like successfully delivering a speech or surfing a big wave, etc.). By visualizing success, you're making success familiar to your brain. By visualizing perseverance, you're making perseverance familiar to your brain. Make clarity, confidence, and execution familiar to your brain using visualization.

The visualization technique is so powerful that athletes use it to learn new skills and to perfect their styles.[43] Studies found that athletes employing weightlifting visualizations triggered the same brain activity seen in actual weightlifting. Even more impressive, those who visualized working out intensely actually increased their muscle strength physically.[44] Exercise psychologist Guang Yue studied both people who went to the gym and those who visualized working out in their minds. After analyzing their physical results, he discovered that those who went to the gym to lift experienced a 30% muscle increase while those who only visualized weight training increased muscle strength by almost 13.5%. The averages remained stable for over 3 months after the tests were done.[45] Think about that!

Visualize Life

What is special about visualization is it need not just apply to specific situations or events. You could visualize the life you desire to lead. Just close your eyes, have your goals in your mind, and

[43] Doty, James R. *Into the Magic Shop: A Neurosurgeon's True Story of the Life-Changing Magic of Compassion and Mindfulness.* Yellow Kite, 2016.

[44] Ranganathan, Vinoth K, et al. "From Mental Power to Muscle Power--Gaining Strength by Using the Mind." *Neuropsychologia*, U.S. National Library of Medicine, 2004, www.ncbi.nlm.nih.gov/pubmed/14998709.

[45] "Conor McGregor - Visualise , Manifest and Realise Your Dreams." *YouTube*, EducateInspireChangeTV, 23 Dec. 2015, www.youtube.com/watch?v=BERpb_6o0fg.

visualize the process of getting there, and then imagine getting there. Enjoy that new life in your mind. Visualize what your experience looks like after having achieved that goal. How do you feel? What do you see and hear and think? What does your routine look like? Your relationships? Make the scenes as vivid and as detailed as possible. Try to feel strong emotion throughout the entire experience. The more real it feels, the more real your brain will believe it to be.

Stealing Dinner from Lions

Preparation, reflection, and visualization are the keys to feeding our confidence. We develop confidence when we prepare effectively. The same is true when we reflect on our pasts and acknowledge the many situations we've survived and thrived through or when we visualize success and overcoming challenges. The three Kenyan men we read about earlier used these three techniques to steal their dinner from lions confidently. They prepared by doing the task many times in the past, including instances wherein they had to ward off severe attacks from the predators. They learned both what went right and what went wrong, and then stood confidently on the foundations of their experiences. They visualized over and over how the situation would have to play out for them to return safely and successfully, and then made sure to be deliberate in their actions.

Although they felt fear and their hearts pounded in their chests, they focused on executing. When they approached the lions, they weren't thinking about failure or about being attacked. They remained laser-focused, sharply attentive and fixated on the objective. Their clear minds were critical for properly handling the situation at hand. Any panic would have fogged their judgment and compromised their decision-making abilities.

Similarly, we must prepare ourselves intelligently. We must acknowledge our strengths, experiences, and capabilities, and then visualize how we are going to thrive through our most important moments.

Positive Feedback Loop

The fantastic truth about confidence is that it cross-pollinates—it breaks all barriers and boundaries when it comes to empowering us in our lives. The more we have confidence in one area, the higher the likelihood we will have it elsewhere. Confidence in more areas of our lives means more courage to pursue other endeavors. If we succeed in delivering a big speech, our overall confidence increases in general. This confidence then gives us the courage to take on other, different opportunities, including ones with no connection to the previous achievement—like learning a new instrument or asking out a date to dinner. As we excel in our lives, we increasingly recognize our competence and our ability to become great at something, at anything—and to thrive.

A coworker who survived cancer once said, "I beat cancer, so what is so scary about an important business meeting? It's no big deal." Having overcome the great struggle with her cancer and having dealt with the high-stake pressure for years, this courageous woman is confident in the face of almost anything else. That is the magic of confidence and courage overlapping in life. It's infinite.

There are tasks in our lives that we lack the ability and competence to perform. However, at least we know we can become competent and perform at our best. We could become great in tennis despite having never played before the same way we became great at math, having once been weak at it. We have thrived once before; therefore, we can thrive again.

TOOL #8:
CHOOSE COURAGE

We cannot exist with confidence by default. Confidence is developed and earned as we excel in life and recognize our abilities to overcome and thrive. The prerequisite for obtaining confidence is courage. Courage is the ability to act bravely in the face of fear, discomfort, or uncertainty. Courage is acting for the sake of doing what we know to be true or right, even when we don't necessarily feel like we want to.

Thankfully for us, courage is not a special power bestowed on a few chosen ones from birth. Courage is an ability—a decision—to act regardless of negative emotions that could be strengthened throughout our lives.

Taking Action

Many times, taking action is easier said than done. Situations like asking out a crush to a date, socializing at your first company holiday party, and pitching a startup idea to investors are all scary. Similarly, decisions like eating healthy, working out, and meditating daily are overwhelming and difficult to start. As much as we would like to "act," many times we can't even bring ourselves to do so when the situation calls for it, let alone execute as confident human beings. We must work with ourselves to encourage action, as well as implement tools and strategies helpful when facing the fear, doubt, or discomfort that arise in life.

Why?

Think about why you should take action in the area in question. Why is it important that you do the act? How will the action bring you closer to your goals and desired outcomes? Is there a higher purpose in what you would like to do? Is this action required for you to take the next step in your life?

If you take an honest look at why you should take action, you will see powerful meaning and value in the courageous step forward. Many times, the reasons for action are practical and obvious. Whether you want to ask your biggest crush out on a date, socialize at a holiday party, or pitch to investors, ponder and remind yourself why you want or need to do what you are doing. Asking your crush out on a first date is essential when you're hoping for an intimate relationship together. Attending your company holiday party is consistent with your goal of becoming closer to your colleagues.

Pitching your startup to investors is the necessary and next step to achieve your goal of securing a Series A round of financing. Decisions like eating healthy, working out, and meditating daily are more manageable when you remember why you decided to do them in the first place. They are consistent with what you want for yourself—to feel good, look good, and become stronger. Remind yourself of these rewards!

Another important question to ask yourself is why you should not refrain from acting. What are the consequences of *not* taking brave action towards what you believe to be true? Well, you may lose your biggest crush to another lover, become an outcast at the office, run out of funding for your startup, and never be the healthy, fit person you dream of becoming. Imagine what life would be like if you didn't take action in any of the areas of life where you want to move forward. How would you feel about yourself? Would you be happy? Would your life have meaning?

Standing still is moving backward, and many times when we delay or avoid acting on what we know to be true, we decline. Our courage decreases, we become less active as individuals, our problems only get worse, and our goals drift further away. We must remind ourselves of this!

Specify

Be specific in what you need to do when taking the next step. Make the actions small and reasonable as you strategize how to move closer and closer to your goal. Just as important, try not to get ahead of yourself. Call your crush and set up a dinner date. Walk into the holiday party and say hi to one person and go from there. Email investors your pitch deck and set up meetings. Eat one healthy meal, go for a five-minute walk, and do mindful breathing a few times. Clearly state what you need to do and exactly what the positive outcome will be.

What Would You Do If You Weren't Afraid?

A great question to ask yourself is, "What would I do if I weren't afraid?" As a human being, it's normal to feel fear about the future, especially if you're trying something new. Although uncomfortable, you should become accustomed to being confronted by terrible feelings like fear and doubt. Make no mistake, they are very unpleasant, and it can be difficult to overcome them, but you cannot let these feelings scare you or discourage you. The Thriver deep inside of you knows these feelings don't define you nor should they affect how you act.

Feeling fear and acting fearfully are two completely different things that come with different consequences. Don't be at the whim of your feelings. Take action after asking yourself, "What would I do if I didn't have this bad feeling?" Your answers could be, "I would ask her on a date," "I would go to the holiday party," "I would set up pitch meetings," or "I'd start being healthier." It is helpful to start talking to your feelings the way you would speak to another person who has a negative attitude and tries to discourage you from doing what you know to be true. "I've listened to you for a while now, and today I am choosing to dismiss you. I will not give you credibility anymore, and I'm going to do what I know to be true whether or not you make me feel good doing it."

Fear

As alluded to earlier, our minds understand how prone we are to damage and pain, and so we experience discomfort daily. While many people call it fear, others call it anxiety and these feelings are code words for "I am scared"—I am scared that I will be damaged and experience pain.

When what we fear objectively poses no actual risk to our lives, the fear we feel is nothing more than a state of mind. As we have seen from the intrusive thought method, our states of mind are subject to control and direction. All of us have the ultimate control over our minds. God and nature gave us control over one thing, our minds. Fear comes in the form of thought. Fear clouds judgment, hurts creativity, weakens self confidence, lessens willpower, and dampens excitement.

When asked what we fear most of us reply: "death," "public speaking," or "spiders." Many of us don't realize how much we are actually paralyzed from fear. Fear is overcome by controlling and directing our thoughts to what we want and how to get what we want. Either our thoughts control us or we control our thoughts. If we have unrelenting thoughts of what we fear most, we find ourselves under the influence of that fear and that which we fear becomes more likely to manifest itself in our lives. Many people claim that fear has suited them well—that their anxiety is directly responsible for the success in their lives and what keeps them focused, prepared, and diligent. This is not the case. Fear is a separate entity from us, and while it may stand by our sides through our achievement in life, it is not the fear that is responsible for our accomplishments. We accomplished significant events in our lives despite the fear. Imagine how much better life would be and what we could achieve if we could live without it.

Fear is responsible for the pain we feel during our paths to achievement. However, this is a useless fear, a fear that only gets in our way. Since the purpose of fear is to protect us, and there is nothing to be protected from, divorce the fear preventing you from your achievement. When we do not divorce the fear, it becomes an all-encompassing worry that fills our imaginations with counterproductive ideas that are hurtful and only promote our demise. They do nothing to protect us. Fear makes life feel like what we fear already happened, and it only delays us from acting on what we know we need to do. We fear to mess up, we fear disappointing others, and we fear to take on new challenges. Vanquish this fear.

Life is oftentimes scary. We each have our physical and mental health to worry about, bills to pay, and responsibilities to deal with. We all have personal deficiencies and must work towards reaching our important goals. Many times, we feel overwhelmed and struggle to move forward. Other times, we completely fall short. Either way, we must move forward towards what we know to be true. It is not as if we are moving forward ignorantly, with no understanding of the risks and challenges up ahead. That would be dangerous. We are not naïve about our limitations and weaknesses, nor where we must improve. We are aware of everything. Therefore, fear not what is to come, just move forward.

Comedian-actor Jim Carrey once said:

> You can spend your whole life imagining ghosts, worrying about the pathway to the future, but all there will ever be is what's happening here in the decisions we make in this moment, which is based in either love or fear... So many of us choose our path out of fear disguised as practicality. What we really want seems impossibly out of reach and ridiculous to expect, so we never dare to ask the universe for it. Ask the universe for it...And if it doesn't happen to you right away, be patient...You can fail at what you don't want, so you might as well take a chance at doing what you love. [46]

Action is never easy or comfortable. Action requires taking a leap of faith into the unknown and holding onto the little courage we have so that we can move through painful feelings, intrusive thoughts, and other obstacles that inevitably meet us along the way. Doing something—anything—is essential, though, because it is the doing that gives us the courage and confidence needed to continue onwards and work harder. Psychologists call it exposure training. It is the idea when we confront that which we fear or that which we are uncomfortable with we become less afraid of it. The

---

[46] Management, Maharishi University of, director. *Jim Carrey's Commencement Address. YouTube*, YouTube, 30 May 2014, www.youtube.com/watch?v=V80-gPkpH6M.

more we realize we can do something, the more likely we will have the bravery to take it on.

As Thrivers, our goal is not fearlessness. Our goal is strength. If we slowly expose ourselves to the things we're afraid of, we will realize we are way tougher and way more capable than we think. As a result, we will be more self-reliant and less dependent on outside protection. We will be able to handle the things we fear and take care of ourselves. This growth is tremendous because we will finally realize we know what is best for us more than anyone else, and we can do what we know to be true.[47]

Remember Brave Moments

Think back to times you were brave and succeeded at doing something new or different:

- When you decided to quit watching television and instead take on reading;
- When you raised your hand in class for the first time and asked an insightful question;
- When you spoke up in a big business meeting for the first time and impressed your boss;
- When you committed to marrying the person of your dreams and now live happily together;
- When you accepted a scholarship to a faraway university and learned to live there healthily and independently.

[47] Peterson, Jordan B. "11: The Flood and the Tower." 2017 Maps of Meaning. www.youtube.com/watch?v=T4fjSrVCDvA&list=PL22J3VaeABQAT-0aSPq-OKOpQlHyR4k5h&index=11.he

Recall, relive, and remind yourself of these moments and realize you are brave. You have what it takes to act bravely.

Dealing with the Past

For many of us, our pasts are like weights on our shoulders. They haunt us and get in the way of us moving forward in our lives. Whether it is because we have hurt and disappointed people or messed up badly, we are not always proud of some things we have done. We have failed, and we have lost people or missions important to us. We have trusted others and were let down. We were ridiculed and attacked. We have had our hearts shattered.

To that, ask—so what? Why must we be slaves to our past mistakes and faults? Why are we chained to who we were and not liberated and allowed to become who we could be?

It is very possible that our pasts still haunt us because there are unresolved conflicts and memories that we did not yet process into our lives. That's okay—visit these moments. Look to understand what happened, why these events happened, and if they had to happen. Who did we become as a result of what we went through? What did we learn? How did we grow? What do we know for the future? Finding the answers to these questions are important because we fear events from the past that we have not yet resolved. When events are unresolved, we still feel vulnerable to them. They are still dangerous to us because we feel prone to fall and get hurt again if we encounter the same situations once more. Once resolved and mastered, we have no reason to fear the past.

When we hurt ourselves, we do not merely ignore the injury and let it rot. It would become infected and worsen in pain. The right action to take is to acknowledge the wound, understand it, and apply healing methods. The injury itself does not bring as much pain as it would if left unattended.

Our pasts are the same. We must discover what still hurts us today and understand why. There are times where we must rewrite the stories we tell ourselves to draw lessons and grow. Take these three examples:

1. "People bullied me in school for years. It was terrible. They made my high school experience horrible."

2. "I wasted a full year of my life working at a failing company. I dedicated my whole life to the company, spending endless hours—even my weekends—working. What a waste of time and energy."

3. "I grew up lonely and unloved. My parents never gave me the attention they gave my siblings. I was always the least favorite child."

Now imagine how they could be rewritten:

1. "High school was very difficult, but it also made me tough. I dealt with relentless bullies and survived. It also gave me compassion toward others. I'd never do to people what was done to me."

2. "I spent a year at a company that eventually closed because we couldn't secure enough capital from investors who seemed overextended at the time. Nonetheless, I gained a ton of valuable experience. I developed my work ethic, I saw what it was like to build a business, and I learned a lot from all the mistakes that we made early on."

3. "I grew up feeling alone and unloved. My parents spent more time with my siblings than with me, and it was hard for me. As a result, however, I became more independent

and self-reliant early on. I learned to deal with life on my own and to find the strength within myself."

The meaning we give something is the reality we come to experience. The stories we tell of ourselves determine the people we become. Meaning and stories are powerful. If we don't carefully choose how we see the events of our pasts, our minds default to habits and patterns of fear and pain. Our life experiences are less about what happens to us and more about how we perceive what happened to us. Therefore, we must change our stories. Pain and suffering become sources of strength and growth. Setbacks and failures become a means of acquiring knowledge and wisdom. Our pasts can teach us a lot, and we must be okay with learning from them to move forward. Once we are comfortable with them, the future is an endless opportunity.

Our pasts do not equal our futures. Our pasts can indeed contribute to the strength and growth we have today, but now, this moment is a clean slate, and we are using it to become Thrivers. What we do now will determine our pasts' influence on our lives. It is not our job to "undo" our past. There is nothing to undo. The more we try to undo, the less we will move forward, and the less we move forward, the more we give strength to the mistakes from our pasts. Undo the past by moving forward. Focus less on the past and our problems and focus more on solutions and the future. Those are what matter most.

Sparking Courage

We must accept we will fail. It will happen whether we like it or not, as it comes hand in hand with progress and growth. The same way we have regrouped and recovered in the past, we will do it again. Courage will force us to do new things, and any initial failure will force us to prepare more and become better and more confident in the process. Courage is like a flame that will inevitably burn out as we encounter the winds of life. Our job is to re-spark the fire of courage and feed the flames by taking deliberate action continuously. Over time, as we gain confidence from doing well in the areas we master, our courage will grow too and spread to other undertakings. Soon enough, our courage will blaze brightly, and as Thrivers we will pursue whatever we desire regardless of how we feel.

TOOL #9:
YOU ARE A LION

The Shepherd and The Cub

One day a shepherd took his sheep to graze in the pasturelands. Upon arriving, the shepherd noticed a cute lion cub sitting alone playing in the brush. When the shepherd walked up to the cub, it looked up at him with adorable puppy eyes. "What are you doing here, little guy?" the shepherd asked. "The lion pride lands are miles away! Are you lost?" The baby cub did not respond but looked curiously up at the shepherd with an innocent smile. As the hours passed and the sheep grazed, the cub played by the shepherd's side. When it was time to go home, no lions from the pride had come to retrieve the cub.

The shepherd warmly patted the cub on his little head and said, "It's time for me to go little fella. I hope you find your family soon!" The shepherd walked away and the cub felt sad. Suddenly, the shepherd felt a little tug on his pants. The cub had followed him and wanted to come along! "You have to stay here and wait for your family, little cub! I have to go home!" The shepherd continued, and the cub followed him once again. Finally, the shepherd realized that the cub had nowhere to go, and he felt terrible for him. The baby cub wouldn't leave the shepherd's side as he walked home. As he approached his house, the shepherd realized he enjoyed the cub's company and decided he would take care of the little guy. He bathed the baby lion, fed him sheep food—the only food he had—and set up a small sleeping area for him amongst the sheep. Weeks would come to pass, and the shepherd continued to raise the baby cub. Over time, the cub fit right in. Every day the cub walked with the shepherd, and each night ate and slept with the sheep.

As months passed, the cub started to grow up and behave like a lion. "No biting!" the shepherd had to tell the lion. "We don't bite. We are friendly." Early in the morning, the shepherd had to teach the lion, "No roaring! The sheep are sleeping! Whisper." When the shepherd would take all the sheep out for morning grazing, the lion would split from the herd and start running freely until the shepherd yelled out, "No breaking from the pack! We stick together! We don't run like that!" The lion then sadly returned to his place in the pack amongst the sheep. This discipline often occurred. The shepherd would train the lion to behave quietly and softly like the rest of the sheep.

Years pass and the lion grows up. Though the lion looked like a powerful adult lion, he behaved softly like a quiet sheep. He ate like a sheep, walked like a sheep, and slept like a sheep. Anytime the lion felt the inclination to veer away from sheepish behavior and to embrace his lion instincts, the shepherd would stop the lion and remind him how to behave like the rest of the sheep.

One day the shepherd, lion, and sheep returned to the pasturelands where the shepherd had first encountered the lion when he was a cub. Suddenly, three lions arrived. The sheep became nervous and frantic, while the shepherd's lion felt curious and excited. He saw other lions! His ears perked up as the lions started to roar, and immediately the shepherd's lion intuitively roared back. The shepherd hushed the lion to keep quiet, and the lion sadly stopped roaring. When the lions started to walk away, the shepherd's lion chased after them. Immediately, the shepherd called him to come back. The lion stopped running in defeat and reluctantly turned back to the shepherd.

The next morning, the shepherd walked to the pen to collect the sheep for the morning graze, and he noticed that the lion had attacked one of the sheep. "No lion! Bad lion! We do not attack!" The lion resentfully took the scolding and walked back to the pen. Ever since he saw the other lions, the shepherd's lion stopped behaving as he had since the shepherd took him in. The shepherd felt distraught. Why was the lion not being himself? Time passed, and the lion kept acting up. The lion ate his food with apathy, wandered aimlessly when with the pack, and never showed any excitement towards the shepherd.

Upon returning the pasturelands weeks later, the shepherd encountered the lions once again. This time, the shepherd's lion jumped up to his feet, stood up tall, and exploded into the most powerful roar the shepherd has ever heard. The shepherd's lion ran up to the other lions, and they interacted a bit. The shepherd looked worriedly at his lion now exposed and vulnerable to all the other lions, but the shepherd's lion looked back at him, nodded his head, and suddenly bolted into the distance along with the other lions.

The lion's heart pumped vigorously as he raced by the side of his lion friends. The sun beamed on his face, the wind rushed through his mane, and he felt alive like never before. He felt happy. He felt a thrilling sensation of freedom and limitless opportunity. Soon the lion reached the pride lands where all his friends and family were. There were dozens of other lions playing, running, and hunting, all together in peace and harmony. He had reached a lion's dreamland. He became a Thriver.

Our Inner Sheep and Lions

As we grow up, people often tell us we are sheep. We hear commands, such as:

- "Behave this way."
- "Do this, don't do that."
- "This is the way we do things."

Sadly, we come to believe that this is true, and we reinforce this belief through the way we behave and make decisions. We tend to show obedience towards those who seem like authority figures to us.[48] Many times, however, these authority figures may not know what is best for us and mislead us. Authority figures could include actual experts like doctors and teachers or perceived authority figures like friends and family members that we admire, fear, or respect. When these "authority figures" dictate our behavior, beliefs, and ability to make independent decisions too much, they take a toll on our self-confidence, self-reliance, and our ability to thrive. Therefore, we must learn to develop our own ability to make decisions and lead our lives the way we believe is best for us.

Inside of us, deep down, we have an inner lion and an inner sheep. In an ideal world, as Thrivers, we would have a healthy balance between the two, where the lion is strong and dominant, and the sheep is rational and keeps us in check. However, these days, we tend to skew towards our fat, fluffy inner sheep, and our lions are weak and starving.

---

[48] Milgram, Stanley. *Obedience to Authority: An Experimental View*. New York: Harper & Row, 1974. Print.

The lions deep inside of us have ambitions and beliefs that we cannot bring to action, and because of these unmet needs, we feel dissonance. We know we want to do things in our lives differently and grow beyond what we're told or how we're taught to live. It pulls at us. Why? Because there is that constant competition between what the shepherds like our parents, our siblings, our friends, our teachers, and our mentors tell us, and the desires, hopes, and dreams of our inner lions. People we respect and who seem to want what's best for us tell us one thing, while our inner lions poking inside are telling us otherwise. This dissonance can be confusing.

On the one hand, the shepherds are keeping us "safe." We don't have to worry about too much or take on too much responsibility. We have others to guide us, make big decisions for us and lead us to the right place. The sheep versions of ourselves are comfortable, secure, and dependent.

On the other hand, we have our inner lions. They have been kept at bay but are dying to break out. Our inner lions wish for freedom, to be given the opportunity to prove their self-confidence and self-reliance. This is the side of us that yearns for the power to make our own choices in life and stick to our beliefs and see our ambitions through.

We continuously have this tugging between our inner sheep and our inner lions. A lion that believes he is a sheep may live to eat and sleep like a sheep, but he is unhappy, and in turn, bad things will happen. A lion who lives like a sheep builds resentment, resentment towards himself for submitting to a life he does not believe to be true, and resentment towards others for forcing him into this way of being.

Remember, both our inner sheep and our inner lions are necessary. The sheep helps us sacrifice selfish tendencies to do what is right and necessary at the moment. The lion helps us put ourselves first and makes us confident and self-reliant. We must tow a healthy balance between the two for us to thrive. Too much sheep makes us weak, and too much lion makes us wicked. Too much sheep makes us submit to the world, and we neglect ourselves. Too much lion makes us selfish, and we destroy everything in our paths, potentially hurting and offending others. To repeat, these days, the voice of our inner sheep is far louder than that of our inner lion, and that is why we will explore how to make our inner lion stronger.

It Starts with Self-Trust

The biggest problem with being a sheep is it's very disrespectful to your inner lion. It is sinful. Let's say your significant other had an important decision to make that would significantly affect your lives together. It could be where you are going to live together, which jobs you're both going to take, or when you are going to start having children. Your partner comes home and says, "I need your opinion on this massive decision." One friend has told her one thing, her mother has said another, her aunt and uncle came up with a third option, her brother offered an idea that is completely out of left-field, and so on. She eventually lists 30 people she has asked already. Would you not feel upset and maybe even betrayed that she's coming to you so late in the game! You'd likely say, "You're asking me last? It's a big decision that will impact both of our lives, and you asked everyone else before you asked me?"

It works the same way with us. There are times when we have big questions to answer or big decisions to make in our lives and before we even check in with ourselves to see what we think or what we want, we run to ask others. This is very disrespectful to ourselves and hurtful to our inner lions.

Think of your inner lion as having a bank account, and every time we defer to others for decisions on important events that affect our lives, we withdraw from the account. Anytime we ask others for reassurance or validation on our choices, we take a toll on the lions inside of us. The opposite holds too. Every time we decide on our own and trust ourselves to make the right choice, we feed our inner lion and deposit in the account. This is for decisions big or small! The smaller decisions like where to eat for dinner are small deposits into our lion account, and more significant decisions like who to marry are big deposits. All these moments in life are opportunities for us to either strengthen our inner lions or weaken them.

When we face a decision, we should stop and think, "Could I make this decision myself without the validation of others?" When we're looking to do business with people, or date, or buy products and services, of course, opinions and reviews from others hold value. The point to take away here is not that we should ignore the advice of others. Rather, we need to be able to courageously decide without the reassurance or validation of others. We must internalize that we have the competence and the ability to make our own decisions and choices. When we do, we develop self-reliance and a healthy relationship with our lions inside. In turn, our lions are more confident to roar when they need to. Otherwise, we're always feeding the sheep, and we'll never be able to use the lions when we need to.

The next time you face a big decision, put your hand on your heart and feel it pumping. Think about what you want and what your heart wants before you ask anyone else. You'll feel something. We have so many decisions to make that affect us. We have choices that result in consequences that we have to live with, that only we will deal with. Yet, we run to other people before we ask ourselves what we want or even think about what we want.

However, this does not mean that we should blindly follow instinct without asking for more information from knowledgeable sources or learning from other different perspectives. If we were to decide whether or not to become partners with someone in business, we should hear what others have to say. People's opinions and thoughts hold value, and at times, truth. Asking our parents about parenting, our religious leaders about spirituality, and doctors about health is smart, as wisdom from those who are experienced makes us more informed and primed for intelligent decision-making. However, we are not going to them for an answer. People deciding for us is very different from us hearing what they have to say and making the decision ourselves. Outside perspectives, neutral or not, are valuable, as we may be missing important details or ideas. However, we should reflect upon ourselves first and see what we believe. Why? Too much advice from too many people confuse us and take us farther away from realizing what we truly want. It's like a broken telephone. The advice and opinions entangle us so much we can't remember what we had initially wanted anymore.

This "confusion" is similar to what happens when we read a friend's answers to homework questions before writing our own solutions. Once we sit to write our own answers to the questions after reading our friend's responses, we subtly and unconsciously write answers similar to our friend's. We don't know if we would have responded the way we did if we hadn't seen their work. Checking over our answers with our friend's responses after we have answered them ourselves creates a very different experience.

Let's say Sam goes shoe shopping with Alex. Alex tells Sam he likes the red shoes. Sam picks up the red pair and analyzes the shoes. Sam didn't even have a chance to look at the rack and see which she liked. Now, she considers the red shoes. Then she looks at others. Will Sam buy the red shoes because Alex told her that he liked that pair most? Or will she look at the others, and then purchase the red shoes because she actually likes them best compared to the others? Or, will Sam purposely not buy the red shoes because Alex told her he liked that pair most and she wants to be different? Or will she buy a different pair because she actually does not like the red ones best?

At the start, Sam should acknowledge his recommendation and still look at the other options herself to make a choice. That way, she truly chooses the shoes of her liking rather than taking the easy way out. Sam may have liked the blue pair to begin with, but Alex's reasonings gave her a change of thought. That's okay! If her inner lioness initially wanted the blue pair, but after reassessing liked the red pair better, Sam could confidently take her change of thought and buy the red pair. She deferred to her inner lioness! The opposite holds true, as well. If Sam originally liked the red pair, but Alex bought the red pair for his sister, it does not mean she shouldn't buy it for herself. Fearing conformity is unnecessary—the red pair is sincerely what she wants. She knows we are bound to share commonalities with other people anyway.

Sam could honestly know the decision is her own regardless of her choice by justifying her decision to herself. Why the final judgment? Why did she decide to buy the pair she did beyond Alex's suggestion? Whether she bought a blue pair she initially liked, or the red pair Alex suggested, does it matter so long as she purchased the shoes she sincerely wanted most?

In his seminal essay "Self-Reliance," legendary essayist Ralph Waldo Emerson mentions how people label others as hypocritical or weak when they change opinions over time.[49]

---

[49] Emerson, Ralph Waldo. *Self-Reliance, and Other Essays.* Dover Publications, Incorporated, 1993.

However, Emerson argues that hypocrisy can be progress—that an individual's changing views signal that the person is growing, changing, and learning. An individual with an opinion that hasn't changed in decades probably hasn't learned anything new. Meanwhile, an individual who truly contemplates and assesses his positions, someone who thinks critically and independently, has the liberty to authentically change views as their opinion is genuine and their own.

We must recognize we are all-encompassing, self-reliant beings. We are not dependent on others to thrive. We have all the answers to our greatest questions inside. When we have issues, doubts, or questions, we should ask our hearts and minds what they think before running to others. Our hearts and minds are sacred. We must respect them, listen to them, take care of them, worship them.

The method of feeding our inner lions starts with building trust with ourselves and building our self-trust starts with making decisions on questionable things without the input of others. We develop positive relationships with our lions when we take action without the need for the confirmation of others. Unless they are certified experts or professionals in the matter, we should refer to our hearts and minds to make decisions in our lives, from what shoes to buy to who we should marry. We are responsible for ourselves—no one else is. We are the gatekeepers and caretakers of our lives.

Although liberating, this truth is daunting to us as well. We enjoy the comfort and security that comes with dependency and relying on others for our decisions and actions. However, to become Thrivers and overcome the struggles we face, we must depend on our hearts and minds to meet our opportunities and opponents. After all, we are the ones who must live with the results and consequences of our decisions and actions. There will be moments where we harness our inner lions to do what we know is true, and our inner sheep will be crying out of fear. We must press on. We must remind ourselves of times in the past where our hearts and minds guided us correctly and allowed us to keep the faith. We will then become self-reliant individuals, with freedom, self-trust, and confidence.

Choosing Beliefs

Becoming self-reliant and strong also means accepting our beliefs ourselves and deciding what we would like to believe and how what we believe affects our lives. Beliefs are like collectible marbles; they can be collected or discarded. We can share and take beliefs from others, we can create our own, and we can throw away the ones we dislike. Beliefs are important, as they influence the way we perceive our existence, but we are not permanently bound to them, and we must remember to keep an open mind, accept that we can be wrong, and abandon beliefs that turn out to be false.

Beliefs Are a Choice

Keeping with the marble analogy, beliefs are separate from us, and we are not forced to believe them all. We can pick and choose which to adopt. People who believe they cannot choose their own beliefs fear them and choose ignorance. Why would they read certain books, listen to certain ideas, and learn alternative ways of thinking if the content may confuse their minds and influence their belief systems?

Others, who recognize that beliefs are chosen and adopted, are open to learning and listening, and then decide what to believe. We may read a book and take 60% of its beliefs and leave the rest.

We may admire a thought leader and not agree with everything she says. This does not mean we should throw away all her work and wisdom! We should take what serves us and leave what does not. If we were indeed forced to believe everything we see, hear, or learn, we would lead terrible and confusing lives, vulnerable to the whims of others and our environment.

What Are Our Beliefs?

Most times, we live by our beliefs unconsciously and do not realize how much our beliefs impact us. However, if we pay careful attention, there are times where we can recognize them and how they impact the way we feel, react, or deal with something. It is our job to acknowledge these moments in time and use them as opportunities to assess our beliefs and either accept, alter, or abandon them.

For example, some people believe in the "evil eye," where essentially one who looks jealously or maliciously upon another can impact a person's wellbeing. Others believe it is a myth, and that only God can influence a person's destiny and spiritual security. Wherever a person falls in this belief, an individual could change his opinion and choose to believe either-or.

Jon & The Evil Eye

Let's take Jon, who grew up in a household that held this belief that jealous people or those who wish badly on others can cause physical and spiritual harm to their victims. Throughout Jon's childhood, his parents warned against hanging out with the envious and delinquent kids in his neighborhood. Due to this belief, Jon avoided all situations that would expose him to the evil eye. He left out the jealous types in his friend group, never inviting them over or engaging with them voluntarily. Whenever they would approach him to see how he was doing, he would respond pessimistically. He'd tell them life is tough or just alright, consciously working not to prompt any jealousy from them. Eventually, his other friends became upset at him, questioning why he avoided certain people in the group.

One day, Jon and his best friend Michael were sitting in the school cafeteria when Tim, one of the kids Jon labeled as "jealous," approached them and sat down. Tim complained about how hard his exams had been and asked how they were doing on their finals. Jon, who had been doing well on his exams, looked nervously at his best friend and then responded, "I'm doing okay. They've been pretty tough, so I'm stressing."

Michael then replied, "Thankfully, I'm doing very well. I struggled a lot at first, but I've been writing index cards in the mornings and then studying at night, and it's working for me. You should try it! I think it will make a difference for you."

Tim sadly smiled and shrugged his shoulders. "Well, good for you. Maybe I'll try it," he sighed, and he walked off.

Jon then looked at Michael, "Why did you tell him that? Don't jinx it for yourself. He might get jealous or upset. That's why I told him I didn't do so well."

Michael laughed. "Jinx it? How would he jinx me? His opinion of me and my life only affects him. I'm studying just as hard for my upcoming exams, so hopefully, I'll do great. And why would I lie to him about how well I'm doing? I feel like that would only bum him out more. At least maybe I could inspire him to take better action and improve."

At that moment, it clicked for Jon. Why would he live by a belief that others could influence his wellbeing? If anything, he should own his strengths and success to inspire others and help them achieve theirs. After all, business people, athletes, and celebrities who proudly show and share their achievements with others serve as role models for people throughout the world and inspire them to achieve greatness.

From that day forward, Jon chose not to subscribe to the belief of the evil eye. He decided that moving forward, he would believe that he is invincible to everyone's energy and instead could focus on himself and even help them with their lives, thereby creating a positive relationship with everyone. This new belief gave Jon the ability to have more compassion towards people prone to jealousy and to help them improve, which would also make them less jealous as people.

As time passed, Jon had moments where his old belief crept upon him. There would be moments where jealous types would approach him, and he'd tense up. But once he reminded himself of his new belief, he felt fine and proceeded accordingly. Over time, he refined his belief further. He believed that no "evil eye" could get him because he had a protective bubble around him that no one could take away except him. However, he chose to believe that behaving like a show-off, obnoxiously arousing jealousy from others, weakens that bubble and does make him vulnerable to an "evil eye" of sorts. That way, he kept himself and his ego in check.

Overall though, Jon grew into a living example for others. Instead of feeding into their misery as he used to under the influence of his old belief, he decided to elevate people who felt down and uplift them with a taste of sunshine.

Cultural, Religious and Community Beliefs

There is no doubt that as members of families, communities, and societies, we are compelled to have certain beliefs and to live by them. While being compelled towards belief is okay, it shouldn't be the only reason we believe an idea. We should internalize why we are choosing to believe. However, these compelled beliefs should not prompt us to stubbornly stick to them or oppose them out of resentment and a refusal to conform. Being a Thriver comes with the maturity of recognizing there are options and being open-minded when deciding what is truly best. Many times, a Thriver is willing to give in on certain areas for a perceived greater good, even when it's not what is best for this moment.

Mentors, Role-Models and More

It is appropriate (and strategically sound) to have a small group of people who are in touch with their inner lions and who know your inner lion enough to guide you and check-in with you. Whether they are our mentors, role-models, friends, or family members with whom we have a strong positive relationship, it is always good to have people we can go to for input, advice, feedback, and perspective. Make sure you compartmentalize where you receive your advice and from whom, as a person who is a master in one domain may not be in another. Know in advance who you speak to for what subjects. You may confide in one person regarding business matters and in another regarding relationships, religion, or health. Either way, it is always beneficial to have honest confidants to speak with and who can ensure that we are in check and that neither our lions nor sheep get out of hand. It is likely important that your friends and family like the girl you are going to marry. It is likely important that your husband supports the job you are accepting. Do not overdo asking others for insight and advice. For every few decisions you make with the help of others, work to make significantly more by yourself.

Thriving Amongst Shepherds and Sheep

Our goal as Thrivers is to thrive regardless of where we are or with whom we surround ourselves. We are working towards having the power to have shepherds and sheep surrounding us, and yet remain strong, self-reliant lions. We should not have to run away and hide to be lions. We can be lions whenever we choose. It all starts inside. We don't have to move out, or travel, or get married, or go to college to be independent. We need to commit to being lions, always working to feed our inner lions and taking every opportunity to strengthen ourselves.

Separating yourself from shepherds and sheep helps, as does not being within the vicinity of people who poke at your lion. However, that's a cop-out, an excuse to take the easy way out, which takes away all the good that comes with community and family. There are many sheep, living their independent lives in their sheep apartments away from home.

Create your energy independent of your environment. Remind yourself that you have a protective shield that can block any attacks on your inner lion. Don't let your home, work, or any environmental or emotional life affect your actual life. You can enjoy and live a beautiful life in your home, office, or wherever you are. Become energetically strong and independent. Realize your lion is inside and thrive amongst the shepherds and sheep.

Resist Sheepish Inducement

Another challenge is when people pull us into their own sheepish conflicts and trigger our sheepish feelings. One day, our lions will be strong enough and we can engage with sheep leaving our lions unscathed. In the meantime, however, it is okay to remove ourselves from the struggles of others if they deplete our energy.

Let's say two people dear to you are caustically quarreling with each other. After many attempts to help, you realize you have no ability nor desire to aid. However, they each continue to come to you to slander the other and bitterly discuss the conflict. If you feel their conflict is beginning to affect your wellbeing—whether in your house, or within your relationships, or your mood when you're with them—it's okay to state that you don't want to be a party to or around their arguments. Remove yourself from their energy. When your lion is strong enough, and you feel ready to deal with the cutting issues of others, you can.

When you're on the other side of the table, stay conscious too! When you're dealing with struggles or problems in your life, learn to become comfortable not sharing your burdens with everyone. It feeds our lions when we learn to deal with struggle ourselves and resolve our conflicts. It feeds our sheep when we choose to vent to others and cannot solve our problems on our own.

Doing What Is Best for Us

Keeping in mind that both our lions and our sheep must be present and healthily balanced, we must make sure that we are doing what is best for both and, therefore, ourselves. After all, we are agents to ourselves. Removing emotions, we must think rationally: What is best for me? Forget what everyone else wants or needs. Ask yourself, "What do I want and need?"

This seemingly selfish way of thinking is selfless because others will flourish more when you flourish. Other people benefit from us when we are doing what is best for us. Our happiness and success will make other people happy and successful. Happy parents give children better lives and happy spouses have better marriages. People who function out of obligation build resentment towards others and they can be miserable to be around.

Real-Time Changes

For those of us who feel a bit overwhelmed or discouraged, we shouldn't be. Even if we have been big, fat, fluffy sheep our entire lives, there is nothing to undo or fix. Our lions and sheep change in real-time as we make decisions. This means if we were sheep our whole lives, nothing is preventing us from becoming lions today. As we trust ourselves more, we will stop associating the past with our current selves, and we will move forward.

As we start strengthening our self-trust, we can rest assured that we are on our way. Just as important as implementing the tools and methods we discussed is believing in ourselves and believing that we deserve to thrive and that we will thrive more with time. We must forgive ourselves for any shortcomings we have today and stand proudly knowing we are currently in the process of rectifying them. We are mortal angels—human at heart, infinite in mind—and we must allow ourselves the time, space, and energy needed to grow. Although we are not yet who we would like to be, we are working on becoming the best versions of ourselves that we could be today. That's all that matters. Patience and compassion are essential. Take a breath.

There will be days where we implement techniques that we have discussed, and they will work wonders and successfully propel us forward. However, there will be other days where we attempt to apply what we're learning, and we will struggle terribly. We should not feel discouraged. We aren't supposed to be on and effective at all times. Certain days we will fail to implement methods perfectly. At other moments, we will implement them effectively, but they still won't work. It's okay. Just journey forward. There are days for battle, and there are days for rest. There are days for winning and celebration and others for losing and recovery. The same way the sun rises and sets, the tide comes in and pulls out, we will rise and fall. It takes courage to do what we're doing—pushing ourselves to grow and contend with forces greater than us. Therefore, we must take our time. We must decide that as long as we are better than who we were yesterday, we are doing great. We must have kindness towards ourselves in this challenging pursuit. We must treat ourselves kindly and show compassion for ourselves the way we would to somebody we care about. We must remember all will pass, everything is for our best, and we will ultimately prevail if we keep journeying forward.

In the Old Testament, when Pharaoh and the Egyptians were pursuing the Hebrews, the verse states: "Pharaoh approached; the Children of Israel...were very frightened; the Children of Israel cried out to God." God then responded to Moses, "Why do you cry out to me? Speak to the Children of Israel and let them journey forward!" God wanted the Hebrews to trust in their guiding light and take action. The heat, the lack of food and water, and the pursuing enemy should not have discouraged them from journeying forward towards the promised land.

We, too, must not worry about everything to come. Rather, we should do what we know to be right at the moment. We are programmed to sustain ourselves, to adapt and evolve as we must. We must trust our hearts as our guides and believe in the magic of our minds. Our hearts and minds are our greatest partners.

We should touch our hearts with gratitude, thanking them for journeying with us on this adventurous life. We should ask our hearts what they want, what they need, and what they know to be true. When we confront painful events, our hearts shatter, and our minds twist and turn. We should not panic. We should support our hearts and assure them that we are there with them journeying to a better place. We must remain grateful for the times we survived and thrived and keep hope and love in our hearts.

When our thoughts become distorted, we should neither judge them nor fear them. We need to quell them and work with them, with a focus on making them strong and properly focused again. We need to encourage our minds to find health and implement the tools we developed to clean them up and create an environment conducive to clarity.

We must stop questioning every comment, belief, thought, and the decisions we make. We must stop questioning ourselves and have a bit more faith. We must stop asking ourselves, "Do I have worth?" This question is disempowering.

What if we replace the disempowering question with an empowering one? What if we ask ourselves, "What is great about me right now?" Trust your inner self to lead you to the right places. The consequence of living your life on your terms is you will be uncomfortable. It is discomforting knowing that no one is coming to save you, or heal you, or direct you, or lead you. But at least you will be the captain of your own ship, and the hero of your own story.

Trust yourself to identify what you like and what you don't. Listen to yourself. Determine your own decisions, your own ideas, and your own beliefs. You are a powerful lion.

TOOL #10:
UNDERSTANDING INTERPERSONAL RELATIONSHIPS

Many times, our inner lions, courage, and self-confidence function differently in social settings. We can all relate to having felt uncomfortable in a social situation at one point or another, especially at large gatherings with people we are not yet comfortable or familiar with. We dislike confrontation, we dread embarrassment, and we hate awkward situations. However, we feel we must attend these events and socialize, or we risk being labeled as introverted outcasts with no social life nor potential for relationships.

Social Creatures

Despite aspiring to be independent, we are indeed social creatures. Therefore, we cannot avoid concerning ourselves with what others think. People's opinions and feedback help us grow and keep us in check. It would not serve us well if no matter what we did, people just patted us on our heads and said we were doing great. We want realness in our lives. We need sincere people who tell us when we're behaving arrogantly or stupidly or when we have something in our teeth. Our social constituents are meant to act as honest, helpful bumpers keeping us on the right path when we're veering.

While we work to care less about what people think of us, we should still value our reputations and work on our images. We also should look to impress others with our competence because, beyond physical desirability, aptitude makes us attractive. Over time, when we influence people enough, our reputations hold value towards our purpose of thriving. We need cooperation from others to achieve our greatest goals. That's one of the reasons relationships are so important. Another reason is that positive relationships are one of the highest determinants of a person's wellbeing. They bring us meaning and comfort and help us stay resilient throughout the challenges of life.

Our Relationship Towards Relationships

There are those of us who are secure in relationships with others and can quickly become close to new people. We are comfortable being vulnerable and dependent on others and vice versa. We do not worry about being abandoned or suffocated, and we enjoy having close intimate relationships with others. We are comfortable approaching others for companionship and support.

Some of us struggle a bit more when interacting with other people. We find it difficult to trust others and would prefer not to be too close or intimate. Dependability and vulnerability scare us, and we would rather keep a reasonable distance and avoid letting people in. We tend to withdraw when approached and don't need to seek comfort from others.

Lastly, there are those of us who feel people aren't close enough to us. We worry about being abandoned or being burdensome to others. We doubt that people like us for us, and we wish we could be closer and more secure in our relationships.

Whichever category we fall into, we all need healthy, positive relationships and must deal with social situations effectively.

Social Courage

For those of us who become nervous in social settings, we must start small. This can begin with initiating simple conversations with strangers who are not in our social groups. We can talk to the man at the gas station. We can ask our waitress how her day is going. When we go to a party, we could make sure to introduce ourselves to two new people. If you're nervous about interacting with others, think about a previous time you successfully conquered a similar social setting. Remembering back to raising your hand in school or speaking to a stranger on the bus are good examples.

Self Esteem

The way we see ourselves and others in relation to us has a significant influence on the way we perceive our status in the social world. We tend to think people see us the way we see ourselves. When our inner lions grow stronger and our self-esteem matures, we worry less about what others think. While this is a clichéd ideal, it holds value. With healthy self-esteem, we both enjoy others and the security within ourselves despite mistreatment, offenses, or contention from people. While we preserve our reputations and our images (they are essential for thriving), we will not base our lives on what others think. We will stand proudly by who we are, accept where we are in our growth process, and confidently share our strengths and interests with others.

As developing Thrivers, our goal in social situations is to either give value to others or learn from them.

Give

Giving to others means leaving people better off than they were when they first engaged with us. We all have strengths, and these strengths should be used to give to others and inspire. Developing expertise like standup comedy makes us valuable to others because it means we can make people laugh at parties and provide them with pleasure. We inspire them when we jump on stage and drop gutsy jokes. All in all, people love when masters of a craft share their abilities with the world. We all have those friends we call for cheering up, great restaurant recommendations, trip planning help, or business advice.

These people bring value to our lives! That's why we love spending time with them. We could do the same, and share parts of ourselves that bring help, joy, entertainment, or inspiration to others. This giving method works with business networking, as well. Rather than focusing on what we want and what we can get from people, we should focus on what we can provide. People value contribution. This does not mean we should live like pushovers and do everyone's dirty work thanklessly. Our goal is to build deep connections with others and earn reputations as useful and valuable people.

Learn

When we feel awkward in social situations, it is because we are too focused on ourselves.

What should I say next? Where do I put my hands? Am I standing clumsily? Is there a booger in my nose?

Putting all our attention on ourselves rather than the exchange we're in makes it hard to enter engaging conversations, which are necessary for social enjoyment. We have all experienced participating in an entertaining discussion where hours passed by in what only felt like minutes. These were conversations where we weren't concerned with having food in our teeth because of the entrancing dialogue or times where we were so interested in who we were talking with that we did not even notice car alarms ringing or babies crying. This phenomenon occurs when we are so engaged that our inner critics and egos turn off. We are not conscious of what is happening inside of us or around us. We're in the experience. We are engaged.

When in social situations, we should focus on the person we are talking to. What can we learn from them? What is a topic of mutual interest we can bond over? There is nothing more enjoyable than an interesting discussion with someone with whom we share values or a mission. Look for opportunities to hear from others and learn something new. Don't look to impress or brag. Approach the person with genuine curiosity. There is much we could learn.

Stay Light

Many people believe acting serious in social situations makes them seem confident, secure, and impressive to others. While accurate at times, acting seriously is neither attractive nor inviting. The more serious we become, the heavier we feel, and the colder we act towards others. In reality, people like us when we simply are ourselves. People reward competence and confidence.

Assertiveness

When people poke at us—especially fellow lions—they are pushing the limits to test our resilience and to see what we're made of. Social interactions can be about sizing up others, and many times a person's comments are meant to irritate. The way we respond depends on the type of jab. Some poke fun at us, to which we should respond accordingly with a prod back. There are others, however, who are attacking us. These are personal assaults, private or public, that cross a line. When these occur, we must confront the individual and make it clear that we do not like and will not tolerate such comments. Whether or not they concede is irrelevant. We must make it clear that we will not be abused or taken advantage of.

Categories of People

It is important to recognize that we will encounter many different types of people in our lives. Identifying and understanding the various types of people will help us when socializing with others.

Let's say we are enjoying friendly service from a smiling waiter named Al at our favorite restaurant. Every time we come for lunch, Al welcomes us and services us graciously. Eventually, we build a connection with Al. We ask about his background, and we learn about where he's from and even about his interests. Over time, we update each other on how our lives are going. All in all, we feel positive emotion towards Al and the entire restaurant experience.

Now let's say one day we show up to the restaurant and Al is gone. Al quit or was fired. We will likely feel bad, miss him for a moment, and then move onwards to ordering our meals with the next highly trained, friendly, welcoming, smiling waiter. This occurs because the category of friendship we had with Al involved an economic foundation with relational expectations. Al would service us pleasantly and wholeheartedly, and we would, in turn, have an enjoyable experience and leave a generous tip. This understanding mediated the goodhearted connection between us. This does not mean, however, that our relationship with Al wasn't sincere. Quite the contrary! We were sincerely interested in Al and his life, and he too sincerely enjoyed our company and conversation. Nevertheless, we were not friends with Al outside of the context of the restaurant. Within the four walls of the restaurant, Al was our friend. Outside of the restaurant, however, Al was not present. We were not looking to help him move into his apartment, nor answer his call in the middle of the night. Al was a friend in context, and he fell within a specific category of social relations.

There are also categories of people within our closer circle, people with whom we share a more intimate relationship. Some people genuinely love us for us and want to spend time with us to be with us. They usually provide us support and interest and give us feelings of positive reinforcement. Others also love us for us, but they poke at us, as well. Often, they are only innocently poking fun, and they mean well. They tease and test us, but we don't mind.

There is another category of people who are friendly and cordial, but they poke at us to irritate us. Again, they mean no real harm, but they annoy us. One moment they could be buddy-buddy with us, quite superficially, and another minute insulting us. We tend to avoid these people. Should we have to engage with them, we try to keep it short.

Most terribly, there are some who actively seek to hurt us. They prod at us and intend to shake us. They may talk badly about us in front of us or behind our backs, but we know they have it out for us.

There are also people who only interact with us when they need something or want something from us. Sometimes, they are using us for our resources and are strictly looking to benefit from the relationship. Other times, these people sincerely look to us with respect and trust us to provide them the help they need. Many times, this is a compliment to us and our abilities, and the value we bring to these people, while not always shown, is much appreciated.

If someone walks up to us at a party and insults us, we shouldn't suddenly feel upset, insecure, and resentful. Does the person fall under the category of people who innocently poke fun without meaning harm? Or is the person malicious and intends to hurt us? Either way, why should it affect us? We expect to encounter people in these categories; therefore, we can move forward despite them.

Thankfully, we have many positive relationships across groups, and so we should not allow a single interaction to seriously affect us. We have many people in each category that feed us in different ways, and so one comment or one act from one person should not affect us. If someone we respect or love insults or attacks us, we will feel it worse. Should this happen, we should entertain the notion that we may have something to think about or something to confront. Valuable feedback and criticism from others fall under this category. However, in the case where an attacker attacks us just to get a rise out of us, we should feel okay knowing that the person falls into the category of people who attack. It is not us, but the person that is the problem.

Scenario #1

After weeks of not speaking, Tim reaches out to Steve for help with his accounting.

Possibility #1

Tim is only using Steve for help. He is not a true friend.

Possibility #2

Tim admires and trusts Steve's expertise and competency in the subject. He feels comfortable enough to reach out for help.

Scenario #2

David tells Joseph that his red shirt makes him look like a giant tomato.

Possibility #1

David is looking to embarrass and offend Joseph in public. He is mean.

Possibility #2

David is only innocently poking fun at Joseph. He loves Joseph and figured he could handle the joke.

The next time a long-lost friend reaches out to you for help, ask yourself: *Is this person using me or does this person feel that I can help him?* It could be a compliment to you.

When someone at a party walks by you and calls you a name like "loser," reflect: Am I a loser? Does this person mean that, or is this person just in the category of people that pokes fun?

We will encounter all kinds of people. The key is that we find some diversity. If we have just "pokers" or "attackers" in our lives, we will be miserable. We need a healthy mix of real friends, pokers, attackers, and everything in between to be happy with our social lives.

Dealing with a Poker

The best way to deal with a poker is to poke back. This could be an improvised joke on the spot or a preplanned response set in advance. If you walk into a party and you know someone is going to comment on your shirt or your facial hair, plan in advance how you would like to respond. It could be a funny response or an amusing joke back. Either way, don't respond to a poker too seriously, or there's the risk of coming off as soft and as someone who can't handle a joke.

Dealing with an Attacker

When a person attacks you, there are three main ways to respond. The first way is not to respond at all or walk away. This response is for people with malicious intent who mean absolutely nothing to us. You can ignore them because there is no desire for you to resolve or reconcile the issues between you two. When you refuse to respond or spend any energy dealing with them, you show that they are worthless to you and a waste of your time. You don't even give them the basic respect of acknowledgment.

There are other times where an individual you respect, love, or care about attacks you, intentionally or unintentionally. Either way, this is a person you will likely interact with often or at least have to deal with again (a sibling, parent, friend, etc.). There are two ways to respond to this type of attack. The first is not to react or brush it off, intending to confront the person later privately. These types of instances tend to occur in a public forum and the attack is usually quick or minor, and then the person moves onto the next point in the conversation. Later, in private, you can approach the person and say, "I didn't like the way you insulted me in public earlier. It was mean and hurtful. I would never do that to you. Please don't do that again." Generally, over time, this response leads the attacker to gain respect for the person. During the first handful of confrontations, the attacker may brush off the assertiveness and say, "Chill out, stop being so sensitive, what's the big deal?" Repeating the assertiveness, however, will chip away at the attacker and the attacker will get the point. Let them know: "I am telling you I don't like it, so stop."

Another way to respond to this type of attack is to react assertively at the moment. It is possible that the attacker in this scenario is a sibling or a friend who may have inappropriately criticized you in public, and there is an apparent and lingering discomfort after the comment. This is an excellent opportunity to respond back and publicly put the person in their place. This is not always easy, as we tend to get blindsided when someone throws an unexpected jab at us in public. However, when deployed successfully, this strategy is powerful.

The reason we must stick up for ourselves is that when we don't, we build resentment towards ourselves. We return to our homes at night and regrettably ponder how we could have responded better. We lay in bed, wishing we stood up for ourselves. Over time, if we do not assert ourselves, we become afraid of confrontation. We cannot negotiate salaries or sales in business, we cannot ask for what we want in life, and we are prone to be taken advantage of. We must learn to assert ourselves. This includes when we are compelled to do something we don't want to do.

Doing What We Don't Want to Do

One summer Sunday, Jane and her mother had a wedding to attend at 6 pm. She scheduled her hair appointment for 3 pm because she planned to go surfing earlier in the morning with her boyfriend whom she hadn't seen all week because of her busy work schedule. When Jane was getting ready to leave, her mother called and told her to take an earlier, 11 am appointment. Her mother sounded busy and aggravated and pressed Jane to take the appointment, but doing so would disrupt Jane's entire day and make it impossible to go to the beach, let alone surf with her boyfriend as planned.

Scenario #1

Jane whined about having her plans disrupted and yelled that it's not fair, but her mother didn't budge. Jane frustratedly slammed the phone and screamed. She called her boyfriend, complained about her mother's inconsiderate request, and canceled her plans. She took the 11 am appointment and felt upset for the rest of the day.

This scenario resulted in two upsetting realities. First, by whining and complaining to her mother, Jane only encouraged her mother to push the request onto her further. Her mother's objective was to get what she wanted, and she wanted Jane to take the appointment. Jane's mother knew that if she pushed hard enough, she could get a whining Jane to do as she was told. Secondly, and most, unfortunately, Jane failed to assert herself. She did not maturely defend her plans. Instead, she regrettably submitted to her mother's will. This resulted in resentment towards herself and her mother for putting her in a position to do something she didn't honestly want to do. At the wedding, Jane is upset and cold toward her mother. Her mother tells her to grow up.

Scenario #2

Jane respectfully tells her mother that she sincerely wishes that she could help her with her stressful day and take the earlier appointment. However, Jane says she has already committed to surf with her boyfriend and that she cannot cancel. She explains that she planned the day with her boyfriend days in advance and that it's important to them. Consequently, she is not willing to switch appointments. Jane politely rejects her mother's request and asks her if there is anything else she may need help with. Bothered, her mother says no and hangs up. Jane, however, finishes getting dressed and goes on with her day.

In this scenario, Jane is mature as she presents her case to her mother. She calmly explains why she is deciding to keep her hair appointment and why she is not willing to take the earlier slot at the salon. In other circumstances, she would have been happy to take the appointment and make her mother's life easier. Although her mother is upset at the moment, at least Jane will enjoy the special day she had planned and will retain feelings of love and kindness for her mother. Her mother sees Jane is respectful, mature, and assertive, and deep-down respects her for it. Their relationship only grows healthier from the interaction.

Scenario #3

Jane feels terrible about her mother's situation and tells her that she will call her back ASAP. She contemplates the situation and ponders if she's willing to sacrifice her plans to help her mother. After some thought, she decides she is, and she tells her mother she'll make the switch.

In this scenario, Jane did not want to cancel her plans to take the earlier hair appointment. However, she contemplated the situation and determined that she was willing to make her mother's life easier. Although she did not want to take the appointment, nor did she have to, she voluntarily did, and there was no resulting resentment. It was a clear and conscious decision for her.

Roles & Responsibilities

When we feel forced to do things we don't want to do, we automatically build resentment towards the people who push us into the situation. The only exceptions are when we decide we are willing to fulfill the request (like Jane's third scenario) or understand that the chore is our responsibility to complete. As another example, take Jack and Kylie. They are newlyweds who recently moved in together. As they settle into their new apartment, they divide and delegate roles and responsibilities. They determine that Jack handles duties like bringing up the mail, taking out the trash, and doing the dishes. Kylie's responsibilities include grocery shopping, cooking dinner, and cleaning the apartment. Because these were mutually agreed upon responsibilities that Jack and Kylie voluntarily took upon themselves, they feel no resentment when doing their respective tasks, whether they like the jobs or not. There are nights that Jack is not in the mood to do the dishes, but he does so anyway without resentment because he understands it is his responsibility. If Jack decides he does not like the responsibility and would like to pass it on, it is a conversation he could have with Kylie.

Let's say part of Kylie's responsibilities includes taking care of the plants in the apartment. Week after week, no matter how much Kylie tries to water the plants properly, they wither and die. Finally, Kylie asks Jack if he could take over the responsibility and water the plants. She explains that he would be better at it. Jack gladly accepts. This is a healthy and productive way to evolve roles and responsibilities within relationships.

Take Control

It is time we take control of our lives, even in social situations. We cannot allow people to make decisions for us, attack our spirit, or determine our paths. We must compartmentalize people in our lives and set boundaries. We must make people back off if they intrude into our lives. The only thing that stands between us and our wellbeing is the simple fact that we have allowed our thoughts, emotions, and decisions to take instruction from the outside rather than the inside. We must learn to move forward despite the outside voices that discourage or command us. We must put more effort into listening to the confident and self-reliant voices inside us that tell us what we believe to be true. Only then can we contend with the outside forces.

We also must learn to speak less about our ambitions, passions, setbacks, and worries. People don't always need to know what we're up to, what we're doing, or what we're dealing with. We need to be smart with who we let in and with whom we share our deepest thoughts. People don't need to know our plans to see that we're up to great things. We need to become comfortable not telling people everything. We should not feel compelled to release information about ourselves for no reason, even if someone asks. This is true whether it concerns our health, our relationships, or our businesses.

When we do share our lives with others, we need to ensure we are happy with the state in which we are presenting ourselves. The states we are in will affect the way others grasp what we tell them. If a businessperson is not confident in his business model while pitching to investors, they will feel his apprehension. If a daughter frames a question with doubt or concern even as she seeks reassurance from her mother regarding a decision she made, the mother will respond with doubt and concern. Conversely, if the daughter mentions her decision with conviction, the mother will react accordingly with certainty, as well. We cannot blame others for discouraging us when we share our deepest thoughts, ideas, and ambitions before we are confident ourselves. Any show of doubt, fear, or confusion will affect the way the receiver responds to us.

Who Are We to Others?

There is an old maxim that says each of us as individuals is actually three people: who we think we are, who others think we are, and who we truly are. We obsess over our image in the eyes of others from time to time, and we silently crave immortality. It is a very human thing to want to be remembered, to dream about changing the world, and to be known by all. We look up to our famous role models, the best of their kind who seemed to have left an eternal impression on the world.

The truth is, however, that everyone who changed the world is a hero to many, but a nobody to more. Think of all the statues and dedications found around the world commemorating the influencers and thought leaders across history who we don't even know about. Contemplate the millions of books, films, art pieces, and photographs that were produced to honor the millions of accomplished people whose names you don't know and wouldn't even recognize: all the rulers and warriors and statesmen; all the scholars, philosophers, and teachers; all the billionaires, industrialists, and innovators; all the athletes, performers, and artists. There are millions! And 90% of them mean absolutely nothing to you. Only a tiny handful have their names mentioned in classrooms, let alone our daily lives. Even these individuals are barely spoken of or thought about.

So, what makes them special? Why are they famous if most people don't even know what they did, let alone their names? What did they accomplish?

They influenced their communities. They impacted the lives of the people around them. The statues, books, and paintings depicting the many people we have never heard of mean the whole world to other people—the people who knew them, whether it was their communities, their friends and family, or the people whose lives they touched and influenced.

Take Michael Jordan. He is one of the most famous basketball players of all time. Who had more of an impact on your life, Michael Jordan or your grandpa? Who had more of an impact on your family and your community, your grandmother or J.K. Rowling? Your grandparents may not be world-famous or recognizable by everyone, but they could have had a powerful impact on their friends, family, and communities. That is what is important.

Our goal as human beings is to change the world for the better by starting with our worlds. This means changing the lives of the people near us, like our family, friends and community. While we may desire global fame and power, those who have been the most impressionable to us wait quietly beside us. History's greats are forgotten by the masses because the masses are too focused on their communities and on the greats within their circles.

Then again, history's forgotten greats are never truly forgotten, either. The masses not knowing an individual's historical contribution does not detract from what he or she has done for the world. Just because we have never heard of a certain individual does not mean there aren't others commemorating this person. The person is still a legend within his or her tribe. The person's accomplishments, the lives he or she changed, are all still remembered and relevant.

Our exhausting egos mislead us into anxiously believing that to thrive and achieve success, we must not rest until we do something greater than ourselves. This belief is false. There is nothing greater than ourselves and everything we do has a powerful effect on the lives around us. The questions we should ask are: How can we give to the world around us? How can we bring light to the lives of others? How can we bring out the best in others? We must contemplate the life we dream of leading and take steps towards creating it. We should not concern ourselves too much with how we will get there or what will happen en route, and rather stay aware and open to the opportunities that arise to bring us closer.

ACKNOWLEDGMENTS

The writing and publishing of this first book could not have been accomplished without the influence, love, and support of so many important people in my life, each of whom deserves many words of appreciation. It would be impossible to list every person and their impact on me, so for the sake of succinctness, I will keep it short.

I'd like to thank my dear friend and mentor, Ralph Sarway, for inspiring this book and its content. His friendship, coaching, and the life lessons and stories he's shared have been infinitely influential in my development and appreciation of self.

To my grandparents, parents, and siblings...it is impossible to adequately acknowledge you all in a few sentences, no less an entire book! From being role-models and pillars of our community to giving me unconditional love and values, you have helped me become the man I am today. I thank you from the bottom of my heart.

I would also like to thank my editing team, Kimberly Macleod and Jay Fox, for preserving my voice in this manuscript, and for working on this project on very short notice. They helped ensure the insights herein retain the integrity I have intended.

To Patrice Samara, a long-time friend, and this book's publisher, my gratefulness is immense. Her support has been both consistent and immeasurable. For the last ten years, Patrice has